Quesadilla and Other Adventures

Quesadilla and Other Adventures
FOOD POEMS

Edited by
Somrita Urni Ganguly

HAWAKAL

HAWAKAL

Published by Hawakal Publishers
185 Kali Temple Road, Nimta, Kolkata 700049
India

Email info@hawakal.com
Website www.hawakal.com

First edition August, 2019

Copyright © Hawakal 2019

Cover photograph: pinterest
Cover design: Bitan Chakraborty

All rights reserved. No part of this publication may be reproduced or transmitted (other than for purposes of review/critique) in any form or by any means, electronic or mechanical, including photocopy, recording, or any information storage and retrieval system without prior permission in writing from the publisher, editor, or the copyright holder where applicable.

ISBN: 978-93-87883-71-0

Price: INR 400 | USD 15.99

Who likes eating maach-bhaat every day, daily?

Well, when you're really hungry, my parents told me as a child, you'll eat just about anything.

LA CARTE

L'aperitif
These Literary Meals:
A Brief Introduction
Somrita Ganguly (Providence, USA)   13

Acknowledgements   17

Le plat principal
A Study of Fruit in Three Parts
Jenny Currier (Providence, USA)   21

Rabelesiana
Cristina Peri Rossi (Barcelona, Spain)
*Translated from Spanish
by Elizabeth Rose* (Tucson, USA)   23

Beef Poem
Chandramohan S (Trivandrum, India)   25

Dumplings: a dish of all times
Norbert Góra (Góra, Poland)   28

Gender Neutral
Ardra Manasi (New York City, USA)   29

Ode to Soy
(or, How I Sold my Soul to Seitan)
Ana Gardner (Providence, USA)   30

Bread
Rochelle Potkar (Mumbai, India) — 33

Banana Flower
Sumana Roy (Siliguri, India) — 35

A Kitchen in the Valley
Paresh Tiwari (Lucknow, India) — 36

炒面 | châu-mèing | chow mein | চাউমিন
Somrita Urni Ganguly (Providence, USA) — 38

Shopping
Atar Hadari (Hebden Bridge, England) — 41

Sativum
Felix Green (Providence, USA) — 42

And Annalakshmi cried
GJV Prasad (New Delhi, India) — 43

Carving Salmon
Sudeep Sen (New Delhi, India) — 45

Baba Dokya
Ana Gardner (Providence, USA) — 47

Chai-Sutta
Tapaswinee Mitra (Kolkata, India) — 49

Food Bowl
Rochelle Potkar (Mumbai, India) — 51

Dishinary
Srividya Sivakumar (Coimbatore, India) — 53

Learning Balance Through Food
Shruti Sareen (New Delhi, India) — 56

Thirsty
Anish Vyavahare (Thane, India) — 58

Togetherness *Madhu Raghavendra* (Guwahati, India)	60
jam spread *Aekta Khubchandani* (Mumbai, India)	61
Simple Rhymes for Difficult Times: Dadri, 2015 *Giti Chandra* (Reykjavik, Iceland)	63
The Last Supper *Hiba Ahmed* (New Delhi, India)	65
Tah-dig *Jagari Mukherjee* (Kolkata, India)	67
Making Cheese *Mrinalini Harchandrai* (Mumbai, India)	69
Lost in the Aroma *Sanjukta Das Bhowmick* (Kolkata, India)	71
An Ode to Kanda Poha *Neha Raghani* (Mumbai, India)	73
Cannibals *Atar Hadari* (Hebden Bridge, England)	75
Rice (Scientific Name: Oryza) *Anusree Ganguly* (Kolkata, India)	77
Making Love Through Food *Shruti Sareen* (New Delhi, India)	78
Magic of Flour *Smeetha Bhoumik* (Mumbai, India)	80
Memories of a gourmet *Moinak Dutta* (Kolkata, India)	82

Woman on a Quest for a
Perfectly Round Roti Smeared
with Oil & Chopped Onions
Linda Ashok (Mumbai, India)   84

Indian Dessert
Sudeep Sen (New Delhi, India)   86

Beans on Toast
Nadeem Raj (Mumbai, India)   87

The Big Watermelon
Linda Jummai Mustafa (New Bussa, Nigeria)   88

Sine wave Sultana
Srividya Sivakumar (Coimbatore, India)   90

Sadness Café
Urna Bose (Mumbai, India)   92

Back Home
Pragya Anurag (New Delhi, India)   93

Taste of Childhood
Shanta Acharya (London, England)   95

Ghore Phera: My Homecoming
Shamayita Sen (New Delhi, India)   97

Masala Muri
Kiriti Sengupta (Kolkata, India)   99

Soft Cheese
Anish Vyavahare (Thane, India)   101

Emelia
Rushati Mukherjee (Kolkata, India)   102

Wine for Two
Rohini Sunderam (Juffair, Bahrain)   104

Jollof Battle
Piesie Kofi Babone (Accra, Ghana)   105

At Gol Darwaza
Paresh Tiwari (Lucknow, India)   106

Gelato, Interrupted
Jenny Currier (Providence, USA)   108

Mangoes And Jackfruits
Sharmila Ray (Kolkata, India)   110

Morning Rites
Gabriel Awuah Mainoo (Accra, Ghana)   111

My Coffee
Temidayo Opeyemi Jacob (Ilorin, Nigeria) 112

Mango
Jess Sevetson (Providence, USA)   113

Lorem Ipsum
Paresh Tiwari (Lucknow, India)   114

Time and Tide
Kiriti Sengupta (Kolkata, India)   115

Amin
Madhu Raghavendra (Guwahati, India)   116

Garam Masala
Anish Vyavahare (Thane, India)   118

How Cooking Almost Killed the Cat
Giti Chandra (Reykjavik, Iceland)   120

Nurtured Cravings
Nabanita Sengupta (Kolkata, India)   122

Clarity
Kiriti Sengupta (Kolkata, India)   124

No Love but Good Meat
Linda Ashok (Mumbai, India)   125

Apple
Sharmila Ray (Kolkata, India)   126

Sant Kabir's Couplets
Kabir Das (fifteenth century India)
Translated from Hindustani
by *Somrita Urni Ganguly* (Providence, USA)   127

Eating Rice & Fish
Sudeep Sen (New Delhi, India)   128

Le fromage
Notes on the Editor   131

Notes on the Contributors   133

These Literary Meals: A Brief Introduction

"Morning and evening
Maids heard the goblins cry:
"Come buy our orchard fruits,
Come buy, come buy:
Apples and quinces,
Lemons and oranges,
Plump unpeck'd cherries,
Melons and raspberries,
Bloom-down-cheek'd peaches,
Swart-headed mulberries,
Wild free-born cranberries,
Crab-apples, dewberries,
Pine-apples, blackberries,
Apricots, strawberries; — ...
Our grapes fresh from the vine,
Pomegranates full and fine,
Dates and sharp bullaces,
Rare pears and greengages,
Damsons and bilberries,
Taste them and try:
Currants and gooseberries,
Bright-fire-like barberries,

Figs to fill your mouth,
Citrons from the South,
Sweet to tongue and sound to eye;
Come buy, come buy." ...

"She dropp'd a tear more rare than pearl,
Then suck'd their fruit globes fair or red: ...
She suck'd and suck'd and suck'd the more
Fruits which that unknown orchard bore;
She suck'd until her lips were sore;"

Christina Rossetti,
'Goblin Market'
in Goblin Market and Other Poems (1862)

Food has been at the centre of our literature from the time we started recording our thoughts. Our language is too full of metaphors for eating. The greatest epics ever told – both religious and secular, oral and written – have invested long verses on food: its politics, its culture, and its identity. Turkish delights from *The Chronicles of Narnia*, butterbeer from *Harry Potter*, the elaborate suppers in Enid Blyton, and the mad Hatter's tea-parties have fired the imagination of children and adults alike. When I first read about Oliver eating the peach in *Call Me by Your Name* and, with it, eating a part of Elio, blurring boundaries of self and other, I felt strange passions burning my insides. When Christina Rossetti wrote of Laura tasting the juice of the fruit that the goblin men enticed her with, until she lost track of day and night, hours and minutes, I wished to partake of that forbidden snack. "The whole universe is here," Amit Chaudhuri declared in his poem 'Sweet Shop' talking about the endless rows of sweetmeats in Calcutta's old confectionaries. Food is history. Food is memory. Food is economics. Food is science. Food is sociology, anthropology, drama, poetry, and art. Food, indeed, is a universe in itself.

We are living in times when people are increasingly coming under the scanner for their eating habits as they try to fight against the tyranny of imposed food choices. Many months ago, a poet from Ghana, Oppong Clifford Benjamin, told me, "You write deliciously about food!" This anthology of food poems germinated from that generous comment, but it is also rooted in our present moment, with its unique political urgencies, that provokes us to think about food in myriad interdisciplinary ways.

What does food mean to different people? What role does it play in our lives and our loves? How do different communities consolidate themselves around the axes of food and eating? After all, we not only eat with our mouths, but also with our hearts; or, as Mrinalini Harchandrai says in her poem 'Kitchen Konkani,' "the eyes – 'dollé'/[are] the first organ to ingest food." *Quesadilla and Other Adventures* is a collection of over sixty oven-fresh, hand-selected contemporary poems on food from Ghana, Iceland, India, Nigeria, Spain, UAE, UK, and USA: free-range, reared with care and tenderness, and written with love.

Jenny Currier's 'A Study of Fruit in Three Parts', Jess Sevetson's 'Mango', and Sharmila Ray's 'Mangoes And Jackfruits' take one back to messy tropical summers and the etiquette for eating mangoes. I abandoned all such manners as a child and decided that mangoes cannot be enjoyed until I dirty my hands, mouth, and clothes. As humans, we may try to be domesticated but the animal inside of us wants to pluck the fruit, spill its juice, and suck it dry.

Cristina Peri Rossi's 'Rabelesiana,' translated by Elizabeth Rose, expands the meaning of such passionate eating to the cannibalistic metaphor of making love and consuming the beloved. Sudeep Sen's 'Indian Dessert' further explores these erotics of eating. Srividya Sivakumar outlines an interesting food 'dishionary' in this anthology, continuing to play with words and meanings, while Chandramohan S bravely balances contemporary Indian politics with poetry in his 'Beef Poem'. Linda Ashok in 'Woman on a Quest for a Perfectly Round Roti Smeared with Oil & Chopped Onions' poignantly highlights the stoic everydayness of food, and GJV Prasad's 'And Annalakashmi cried' reminds one, quite pertinently, that food, when stripped bare of its fanfare, is, after all, a luxury that only some can afford, and poetry cannot feed hunger.

The poems in this anthology talk apetisingly about food as an allegory, food as a reality, and food as everything in-between, inviting the readers to a scrumptious literary meal, and taking them on a rich gastronomic journey. Bon appétit!

Somrita Ganguly
Providence, Rhode Island
2019

Acknowledgements

Daddy is a cautious eater, Mummy adventurous. He prefers traditional Bengali meals, she Mexican. Between the two of them they ensured that I grew up eating everything from kochu-shaak-baata to quesadillas.

This book is for Dad and Mum. Thank you for your love and your secret lemon-rice and bread-pudding recipes on which I have thrived for the last twenty-eight years.

My friends from Calcutta, Delhi, Providence, New York City, and Bombay, who have walked with me from Ghalib ki Gali to President Obama's favourite breakfast joint in Chicago, from Parsi eateries near the Gateway of India to hidden Venezuelan arepa joints in Manhattan: you know who you are. Let's spill more red wine from our laughing glasses as we read this book together and cook for one another.

My partner and I bonded over music and mezze. This book is, in part, a consequence of the Bengali, Punjabi, Gujarati, South Indian, Mughlai, Sri Lankan, Vietnamese, Thai, Korean, Japanese, Chinese, Tibetan, Ethiopian, New England, Portuguese, Dominican, Puerto Rican, English,

Italian, French, German, Polish, Jewish, Tex-Mex, Syrian, Lebanese, Greek, American, and Moroccan food that we have shared together. Here's hoping that the future will see a new and revised second edition of this anthology when we have explored more cuisines from other corners of the world.

My family, my neighbours, and my colleagues have always gone out of their way to meet my food cravings. Their generous servings of jambalaya, enchilada, shutki maach, and baklava over the years have been as unputdownable as the poems in this volume. I am lucky to have the best of both: verses and vindaloo.

I am grateful to the Fulbright programme, funded by the US Department of State, for opening exciting doors for me, and showing me what cultural exchange truly means.

(How do you introduce someone to your culture, by the way? I include Tagore, himsagar mangoes, and syrupy, spongy, sweet roshogollas in my starter-pack.)

I am indebted to my publisher for having faith in this project, in these hard times, and deciding to invest in it immediately.

Quesadilla and Other Adventures would not have been a reality without contributions from poets from around the world who believed in me and shared my dream. Thank you, and kudos to each you for cooking up such a storm! Also, cheers to those comrades and connoisseurs included in this anthology who supported my idea since its inception, and added to this four-course meal their perfect, personalized blend of spices!

photo credit: *ediblebrooklyn.com*

JENNY CURRIER

A Study of Fruit in Three Parts

VII. New Zealand

Seven years ago, after hiking alone in the wilderness, I came across an unmanned fruit stand with a donation can and a sign: Mangoes $0.20.

With no one around, I dropped a coin and snatched the last remaining fruit, so soft my thumbs squeezed into its surface. I'd never eaten a mango before,

at least not like this, dissecting it with my bare hands. I wasn't aware of the complexity of its structure—the thick skin, the giant flat oblong seed.

I peeled back the skin hesitantly, until I caught the dripping juice with my tongue, then ripped the remainder with my fingernails, tearing it with my teeth, ravaging its bright orange flesh until my face

and arms were covered in sticky, sweet nectar, and strings of mango hung from my chin.

No, I'd never eaten a mango before.

A. The Fall

I think we know the story by now: humankind separated from God, subject to suffering and death,

all because of a piece of fruit.

When Eve saw the fruit was good for food and pleasing to the eye, and desirable for gaining wisdom, she took some and ate it.

A few generations later came Esau, who sold his birthright to Israel, for a bowl of lentil soup.

And just now, while writing this poem, I ate not one, not two, but three Knead donuts, despite trying to flee from the delicacies of the wicked.

Humanity's appetite(s), it seems, always lead to destruction.

Ω. Revelation

I recently heard a preacher give his Greatest Argument for the Existence of God:

Mangoes.

(The kind, he specified, that require showering after eating.)

"And I'll tell you why," he said. "I have never in my life met anyone who could taste such a fruit and immediately afterwards think, 'There is no God.'"

Here is the good news, translated: every mango is a love letter from God.

Taste and see.

CRISTINA PERI ROSSI

Rabelesiana
Translated from Spanish by Elizabeth Rose

She would love to eat the toes
off my left foot
with a smooth *salsa de cerezas*
and savor sucking each ossicle.

She would roast my right ankle
bound by a delicate string
with the finest herbs.

She would drink my menstrual blood
with a few drops of liquor
and a pinch of cinnamon.

She would brown my fists in the oven
drizzled with plum juice
and sundried currants.

She would fry my thighs in oil
and devour them in the evening
paired with a sweet wine.

Afterward— big as a cow
fatigued from the feasting—
she would begin to masticate
the large, nourishing bolus
satisfied by each swallow.

    If someone reproached her,
having devoured what she loved,
eyes resplendent with pleasure, she would say,
"You are what you eat."

CHANDRAMOHAN S

Beef Poem

(1)
My harvest of poems
Will be winnowed:
If done deftly,
The lighter, shallow poems
Will be blown away,
While the meatier, heavier poems
Will fall back into the tray,
To become the fire
In my belly, like
Beef.

(2)
Mastheads with nausea
Against beef eating
Consider my poems
"untouchable".

(3)
Mastheads
First have vegetarians and non-vegetarians
And then non-vegetarians and beef eaters
On either side of their lines of horizon.

(4)
For some poets
Beef is the
Locus of all the
Food for thought in the world,
Like Buddha's begging bowl.

(5)
When I manoeuvre sharp curves of history
In my rear-view mirror,
I see some trucks overfull with cattle
Waiting at the check points,
Strands of fables
Edited out of history textbooks.

(6)
The pressure cooker's whistle
Is a one-eyed search light:
Hawk's eye on our bellies.

(7)
A dead cow preserved in formalin
Like Hitler's penis in a museum.

(8)
Beef poems adorn various
Poetic forms like sausages-
Cyanide capsules worn around our necks.

(9)
Performances to packed audiences-
And end the poem
With a knockout punch
On their rib-cages.

(10)
Beef nourishes us
through the recipe of a commune.

(11)
Every time the rage attenuates,
I beef up
My poetry.

(12)
My poems are not inert objects
They are verbs of insurrection.

(13)
Beef poems are
Like meatballs of beef
With a label of "handle with care",
Like biting the trigger
Of a grenade.

(14)
Discard a myth
Like a piece of meat,
A vestigial organ being operated on.

NORBERT GÓRA

Dumplings: a dish of all times

It is the taste of history
that connects generations,
it crossed the gates of the past
and crept onto the tables of modern times.

In moments of distant adversity
it was a synonym for luxury,
it cherished socialism,
which took too much,
in times of freedom and openness
it became a gem of national cuisine.

Dumplings – a dish of all times,
sweet, with cheese or meat,
dumpling – a grandma's miracle,
everyone left empty plates.

ARDRA MANASI

Gender Neutral

At your favorite Thai restaurant in New York
you order Drunk Man noodles with chicken
Across the table, a candle away
I flip the menu to match it up
with an order of
Drunk Woman noodles with shrimp
"Extra spicy please,"
To please our taste buds,
this longing on our tongues
we await our gender equal meals.
Ordering another bottle of beer,
you tell me of your first love
who spoke Finnish
a language
with no genders.

ANA GARDNER

Ode to Soy
(or, How I Sold my Soul to Seitan)

I.
Mad-cow disease struck Europe around '96
Fat-cow disease struck my middle-school a couple of years after
When sixth- and seventh-graders started to grow tall and round out
And suddenly everything was apples and melons and grapefruit and omelets
And everyone measured us out in kilograms and radii
Each girl a physics problem with a precise answer.

Over summer it became wrong to eat a croissant
And wanting a slice of sweet-cheese pie became alarming

Aren't you thinking? they asked.

And everyone's eyes fixed on us, burning,
Like some Tolkienesque nightmare
Every time we came too close to a crumb of dough.

Suddenly we were food (bagel-gut, ham-back, drumstick-thighs)
But we could eat none
And we chewed our shame like a celery stick
Its fibers stuck between our teeth

II.
In 2002
The European Union
Announced our fatherland was ready to Ascend

III.
The borders crackled under the weight of western aliens
Nestle, Twix (oh, double the pleasure)
Ferrero-Rocher and Harribo and Chex
An unwinnable dilemma
Pringles were cool but eating them was not
And we could only worship unopened Snickers bars for so long

We cracked, like wafers at the bottom of a book bag
And the all-seeing Eye doubled its watch
Guarding the circumference of our worth

IV.
Amid the influx of sinful goods
Snuck, unnoticed, the bags of desiccated soy strips
An unorthodox alternative to orthodox High Lent

They went, largely, unacknowledged

V.
A struggling local manufacturer figured out that soy had no taste
And could, like a child's character, be molded into anything.

Thus, inconspicuous Fibro-bar arrived, in a modest
label that drew no censure

No one bothered with the ingredient list
Soy was such a bland, harmless figment.

VI.
The greatest con of the century went unnoticed, buried
at the bottom of a girl's bag
Or stacked in plain sight in judicious pantries,
A bar of chocolate and sugar and nuts, grinning in its
soy cloak
Between celery and strips of boiled white fish

ROCHELLE POTKAR

Bread

When the earth diver plunges into a seabed of dough
in the artisanal bakery on the curve of a road
comes bread on palm, waiting for sun,
life-sustainer with sugar, starch, gluten
cosmogonic passovers from cast-iron skillets
azotised and hydro-carbonated
deities of crunchy outsides, moist insides
fermented by lactobacilli
entwined, croissant-like, maple syrup-blissed
drawn from ex nihilo in open-air bakeries
off addictives of bran, rye, legume flour
with salt, this loaf is gazpacho and salmorejo
of hypnopompia
from within the void
life without aysh is without eigengrau
ceremonies of phantasmagoria
states of amorphousness - oral traditions of myth,
thoughts of divinity
baguette giving way to unity; challah to duality, brioche to trinity
bread from the progenitors of sourdough and yeast
passing through worlds - psychic before physical
sound and word, cracking of the Egg

of a life dreamt first.

Old soldiers, bankers, tailors
now grinding grain,
salt-rising, bacterial, cheese-flavored foam,
leavening hope, textured in sweet crust
against the crumbs and croutons of daily kneading
grain rupturing, harvest of coarse flour
stocked in stone-built scent of the walls
bonfires of cold hearths *roti, kapra, aur makaan*
between the crumpets and cupcakes
pretzels, pandesals, eucharistic
the first-light of chimera, warm as broth
baptismal as sun-kissed barely and sedge
bread for the worm, bread for the fish
bread for the rabbit, bread for the civet.

SUMANA ROY

Banana Flower

It arrives on my plate like a patient.
Its appearance the colour of hurt knee,
the peanuts in it like broken headlights,
the coconut scrapings unwound bandages.
I think of it before this impoverishment,
this loss in weight, shelter, and dignity.
Shelter: the maroon boat-shaped whorls,
unending barricades, like walls in ancient forts.
No, to call them walls would be too harsh.
Curtains, then? True, as nomadic as curtains,
but more protective. More affectionate,
like the cup of a mother's fingers on a tiny ear.
Inside them soldiers in saints' translucent muslin,
standing guard, shoulder to shoulder,
as if hiding something, more precious than light.
Inside every soldier is a stick, their only defence.
The cook pulls it out, castrating, then chopping.
So much is washed away: stickiness, generations,
the surprise of births.
All for food, always the gift of error.
In my mouth, a colony of iron, lying comatose.

PARESH TIWARI

A Kitchen in the Valley

Choose the cuts with care. It's an art lost on most except the bloodline of Ibrahim. Their knives are soundless, almost. And the flesh warm still in the cup of your palms. Then the ritual act of cleansing. Wash the meat six times through fresh water. Place it in a brass pot brimming with saffron milk. Knead till the milk seeps into your veins.

sky-full of emptiness
a finger frozen stiff
on the trigger

Dry roast cinnamon. Watch it curl in the heat of the pan. Add cloves. Cumin. Fennel. Brown cardamom. Red chilli. Grind them all and mix with a bowl of curd. Marinate. Leave it for an hour. Put the radio on and pour yourself a glass of wine. Only when Faiz breathes his last, place the marinade over the slow heat of charcoal.

equidistant
from the barbed wires
your bunker & mine

The rice comes next. When you rip open the twine of the sack, the scent of basmati washes over you like first rain, makes itself home in the shelves of your kitchen. Into the folds of your skin. Measure three cups into a deghchi. Pour twice the water. A spoonful of ghee and a pinch of saffron. Split open six cloves over it all. Watch an ocean spume over the pot.

no man's land
the eye of the soldier
not yet dead

An inch thick layer of steamed rice. Over it a layer of curried meat. Repeat, till the clay-pot can take no more. Seal it with dough. Let steam do the rest.

SOMRITA URNI GANGULY

炒面 | châu-mèing | chow mein | চাউমিন

        <n. stir-fried noodles>

In Calcutta, chowmein was ubiquitous in the '90s in urban Bengali households. Through a strange semantic change, the word was shortened to chow: the stir-friedness of the mein gaining precedence over the meinness of the mein in the foreign tongue.

Maa made white chow for Sunday breakfast when there was not enough time to fry luchi or porota in the morning. She usually slept until 9 a.m. on Sundays.
        <her only luxury for many years>
White chow was white:
        <like a white flag>
        <like off-white handmade paper>
        <like my Jewish-Christian-white-American partner's skin>
Wheat noodles gently boiled in hot water and then lightly fried in vegetable oil, with some chopped onions, salt, pepper, and sometimes an egg on indulgent weekends. No sauces. No food colouring. No pretensions. Simple.
        <like most middle-class Calcuttans>

Baba brought home chicken chow doused in chili sauce from local eateries on some Wednesdays, for dinner, when we needed a midweek break from our bitter gourd
bottle gourd
silk gourd
apple gourd
ivy gourd
pointed gourd
Unexciting, unexotic routine.

My friends and I took veg-chow with ketchup for lunch, at least once every week, when we were in high-school. The chow turned cold in our tiffin-boxes but there was fire enough in our sixteen year old hearts to make up for congealed noodles. Our steel tiffin-carriers were so desi that I am embarrassed of them now in my present <no-plastic-pontificating-yet-plastic-tupperware-using> first-world situation. Back then nothing could embarrass us.
    <youth has no shame>
    <shame comes with age>
We would surreptitiously pass our ugly, eco-friendly, cold tiffin-boxes around, way before lunch-break, feasting on chow while the teacher droned on in the class about the cardiac system or tectonic plates.

A lot of my childhood seems to have been spent watching <with doleful eyes> roadside food-cart vendors creating magic with chowmein. Maa and Baba always denied me the exquisite pleasure of eating anything from the roadside. I still remember Maa asking me in wonder and in exasperation:
    <if not in complete shock>
"How on earth is that dirty thing from the streets more appealing to you than a healthy fruit salad, or brunch at Flury's, or Peter Cat?"
    <the forbidden has always been more tempting, Maa, always>

The Bengali-Chinese chowmein was such a big part of my growing up years that when I went to Beijing for the first time in 2010 and had 'authentic' Chinese noodles, I felt the ground beneath my feet shaking in anger. I felt cheated, betrayed, let down, and decided <quite petulantly> to live on burgers and fries for the rest of that trip. To a seventeen year old me, Bengali-Chinese was the real deal. Everything else was a sorry simulation.

I tossed some noodles in a wok for breakfast this morning. It was nothing like the chowmein of my childhood. I used organic semolina-based Italian angel-hair pasta,
<and not coarse wheat noodles>
free-range brown eggs,
<which the roadside vendors of Calcutta probably have no clue of>
extra virgin olive oil,
<instead of what dad used to call "C-grade, inedible, dubious white-oil">
<which was always used very generously by the aforementioned vendors>
and shriracha
<in place of ketchup>

And my plate of East-George-Street-Instagram noodles turned out too hipster to be humble like old Calcutta. Yet, the smell of fried eggs mixing with the mein felt closer to home than anything else has in my last few years in Rhode Island.

<I took my chowmein and my childhood for granted>

ATAR HADARI

Shopping

Shopping that one time
when she came to stay for a week
by the sea and we finally got to shopping
on day three and she didn't eat everything
before going a day early-

It was nice, going with someone
saying "Look, here's who I'm going with
to the shops, who I'm buying cornflakes
next to, this is who pushes the cart
when I'm tired or shyly asks
if we can have sticks of butter with bread,
can we buy cakes that will not last?

Later, so much later,
all that shopping remains unopened,
uneaten though we fingered last crumbs
and threw them down the drain.

Over the parking lot
where we walked pushing steel trays
our ghosts clasp their silken fingers
to the ends of their open ungovernable, open hands,
and snatch a swift air kiss,
mwah, mwah, though they no longer know
where the other lives.

FELIX GREEN

Sativum

For my sister, Claudia, who gave me the idea for this poem

      I find you hiding, white and rosy fresh,
amongst like friends, both fine and plump. So stuck
and clad in smooth revealing dress, your flesh
is firm, so, firmly grasping you, I pluck.
      To no caress will you your heart release
and so I strike, pound, pierce as with a knife.
Your robes now flung aside that earlier did tease,
your body crushed, you render up your life.
      You linger still, your perfume on my breath,
your wetness here that to my fingers clings,
and to my tongue your fiery taste. In death
you linger still, and I your praises sing.
      And were I Dracula, I cannot lie:
for you, O Garlic, 'twould be sweet to die.

GJV PRASAD

And Annalakshmi cried

Every morsel you waste
Adds another drop of tear
To Annalakshmi's eyes
As she mourns by the river
My grandfather said

An American friend said
His mother made him eat
By asking him to imagine me
Starving in India
Or Africa

But how would that have helped
I asked him
Only made you bigger and stronger
To put me in my place
He didn't know
He had never asked his mom
And she was dead now
And in any case
This Indian didn't look like
He ever starved

Maids used to bring lunch
For the rich kids in class
And the smell of eggs and oranges
Still reminds me of school
Curd rice of home
While I longed for samosas and coke

We went without sugar
For a year or two
And rice was difficult to find
The green revolution
A distant dream
Not yet a nightmare

They poured milk into the seas
Elsewhere
And let grains rot in the fields
The same world I would think
And when they did send
Some across
We hated them

I remember when potatoes
Meant a feast
We were the privileged ones
Whose dustbins others
Would forage and envy
The one who got more
Snatching it from dogs

Source locally they say
Sustainability they intone
Where there is clean water
And fertile fields
Some can do so
Because they can
Others will do as ever
Because they can't

SUDEEP SEN

Carving Salmon
Cinematheque Restaurant, Jerusalem

>The besotted fish,
>   finless in its flight,
>stares dead straight

>at Mount Zion,

>from the ochre stone's
>   unsure solidness.

>The waterless valley
>   dips between
>Mishkenot Sha'ananim

>   and The Old City
>inviting us
>   to swim through

>the unsure tide
>   and times,
>time that ticks

in uneasy peace,

just like the peace
  destroyed by pieces

of broken fins,
  arrows, missiles,

bones, and, fate.

ANA GARDNER

Baba Dokya

Chai and goat's milk
An unlikely mix
Unless you live in the Balkan foothills
Off the main road, up the cliffs
In a two-room log cabin hidden by juniper trees

Chai substantiates into clay pitchers on the kitchen table
Like the holy flame on Easter midnight
You don't ask where it came from; it just is

In the mornings when the brass kettle whistles
The sky outside is close and crisp
And dew sticks to your woolen socks

Cold and hunger prickle as you
Breathe in the sunrise
That smells like wet earth and deer afterbirth

Chai and fresh goat's milk wait on the table
Both warm, and menacingly unpasteurized

A chunk of steaming bread completes the holy trinity.

Goat's milk and chai:
Sounds like a hipster soap
Unless you're an old grandfather born in the age of transhumance
Born to a womb of earth and wheat
Into skin painted by sun and scythe scars

Chai kept sunstroke at bay out in the pasture
Packed in a leather bag by a mother
Who spoke her love in spices and warm dough

The milk of eighteen goats marks your passage.
The eighteenth finds you, stooped in the same stable
While another young dochka greets the morning

The sun writes lines into a new skin
And the mountaintop breeze punctuates it with goosebumps.

You bring the fresh goat's milk into the kitchen
Next to the clay chai pot that's never cracked.

Together, they measure out our generations.

TAPASWINEE MITRA

Chai-Sutta

He smelt of chocolates and
roasted brown marshmallows,
a shade of brown, the tint of my skin.
Marshmallows in his skin-
roasted to my skin,
pale marshmallows roasted brown.

The chai we drink at the *dokan*
outside our university,
is a similar brown,
brown of my skin–
like pale marshmallows turned brown.

He drinks tea of a different shade–
the color of his lips;
his lips, or the shade of lipstick I wore when I had
kissed him.

The *sutta* we dragged with Shyamal da's chai
served in little clay pots,
left a sweet after-taste on our pink lips.
"Godam Garam, was my first cigarette," he declared.

Sweet cigarettes with salty tea,
cigarettes, occasionally stolen from his father,
or a sly gift from a friend.

I once made black tea for him;
"*Raw chaa*, we are out of milk."
"How do you make tea without milk?"
"How do you drink noon-chai, tea without sugar?"

He smelt of chocolates and marshmallows.
Taking out a bottle of attar from his pocket,
he rubbed some on my neck,
muttering, "Applying attar on a woman in public is haram."
I smelt of chocolates now too, but not of marshmallows.

A procession marched through the gate:
A shrill "*Hum kya chahte?*"
An echo "*Azaadi.*"
Walking the procession together, I asked
"What do you want *Azaadi* from?"
"From *raw chaa*, definitely! And you?"
"From you wanting *Azaadi* from *raw chaa*."

*Noon Chai: Salted tea, drunk in Kashmir

ROCHELLE POTKAR

Food Bowl

Where else, if not this land scattering seeds to wind,
waiting for the shaft of ripe sky harvesting crops of rain?
Take from the sky if it gives
the ground in falling water levels, bullock over till,
credit from middlemen, seeds, ads for pesticides, poor irrigation,
arsenic and mercury - a cancer train Bhatinda to Bikaner.

Alcohol on empty stomachs
Take babies with no brains, the resistance of pests, and friendly insects dying.
Take cotton disembarking in clouds in crucifix branches,
hills like salt pans in the ritual of GDP,
no gunk on biodiversity: soil or species.
Take the backstory of a tiffin,
law into your hands, a sip from the tin.

Under colonial-keeping these were just *injuries*.
Take the widow, her debt n' inheritance.
No marriage for her - indentured servant.

Take late rain from a ditch at a point
the baton changes hands off the green revolution...

Take hundred spoons from a bowl, in the highest-
stressed profession.
Our land exporting cereals, with images of India Gate, Taj Mahal,
and a woman's round face like a plate. *Annapurna devi*
four hands to give grain, hold vessels, ladles.
Take her god husband - like the government – telling her
life is an illusion,
Take her anger, churn of earth to barren.
Hunger waking in bodies
even the Buddha needing meal before illumination.

Take a toss of the last coin,
in the gamble of the huge gap
the fact that Annapurna *devi*
has still not returned.

SRIVIDYA SIVAKUMAR

Dishinary

A for asafoetida: Reminds one of mothers and hot fragrant kitchens.
B for bhindi: Ma stuffed them with spices and heart. We ate with nothing but our fingers and joy. Years later, friends ask me if she still makes them.
C for coffee: Filter. Finicky. At times, a wakeup call. Most times, a lingering cup of love.
D for dal: At weddings, it is served with a drop of ghee and a dash of salt. Sublime warmth.
E for eggs: Democratic, gregarious; it mixes with everything.
F for fish: Swim upriver for survival but end up eaten anyway. The Bombay Duck is a fish. As is meen curry. My sister is a fish- a rose- spectacled Pisces.
G for ghee: Lubricant for tired bones. Poured on funeral pyres. Enhancer of pretty much everything. Try it in your bullet coffee, maybe?
H for hummus: He makes it the old-fashioned way; orders the tahini off the net. Feeds me with fingers slick with olive oil.

I for ice cream: The suspect agent orange stick. The simple dusty corner shop that smiled.
J for jalebi: Sour-sweet, deep-fried, your arteries cry but you love it. For meals and snacks.
K for kozhambu: Deeply glistening, slow-cooked, tamarind jaggery sticky seduction. Eat with rice and g for Ghee.
L for love: Essential ingredient in cooking. Or so they say. L also for lemon. Fades dark spots, offers fair skin. Make you marriage-able.
M for marmalade: Rind feels fine on toast and tongue. Bake, slather, eat plain- it's all good.
N for nuts: No pecans for us. We like walnuts and cashews and golden raisins. As a Diwali gift and for New Year wishes. As a healthful snack. But we eat too many.
O for orange: Contrary to popular belief, my king of fruit. Eaten plain. Better cold with salt and pepper. The inside of an orange peel is the albedo.
P for pickle: Dark red, red chilli, chilli and lime, lime tang. Tender green pepper in brine, sarsaparilla in hot salt and chilli, mangoes cut to size in oil and mustard.
Q for qubani ka meetha: Think apricots and Hyderabad. Sweet dish topped sometimes with another N we like- almonds. Poetic nights and promised parties. Exotic, excessive. Essential.
R for rasam: Comfort food. Healer of cold and cough. Light enough to drink, heavy with memories of home. Also, H for honey. What I don't call you.
S for sweets: You are your sweet tooth, I'm told. Sweetmeat is an oxymoron.
T for tea: Social drinking, sibling style. Crush ginger for great flavour. Serve in small glasses or pretentious delicate cups. Refreshing in every way.

U for upma: Breakfast staple. Light on the stomach. Heavy on savings.

V for vegetables: Gorgeous, flavourful, plenty. Nice in a salad. Not so nice in a cake. But then, there's always carrot.

W for waffles: Mountain memories, drunken nights and amused cousins who've tasted better.

X for Xmas cookies: Ditch them all for rum held together by flour and called a pudding.

Y for yogurt: We call it curd. Sugared, it brings good luck. Plain, it rounds up lunch and dinner. Good as a hair mask and for the face.

Z for zebra cake: A crowd pleaser, perfect for a great reveal or to just show off.

SHRUTI SAREEN

Learning Balance Through Food

Salt is an essential requirement in food.
So, heap it up. No, not so much as to become
too much! You are cooking vegetables, not salt, you see.
Salt is what you call a spice, or a condiment.
It can make you, or it can break you. That's the thing with salt.
And the thing with hot crackling spluttering oil too. And with sugar.
And with a zillion other things. Heck, it's the thing with cooking itself.
How did our ancestors live without fire?
Cooking is vital but too much only leaves you with charred remains.
So, how much do you need of a good thing?
Are you making gobhi-aloo or aloo-gobhi?
Do you want to balance the green with red and yellow bell peppers?
What mix of sociology, history and poetry in a literature PhD?
How many poets is too many poets? You need to decide.
Of course, you may have milky sugary tea. I prefer it without.
Then there are those who leave the tea leaves out of the tea and make it herbal.
What proportion vodka in a glass of orange juice? Or vice versa.

As a Facebook meme said, a balanced diet is red wine with white,
milk chocolate with dark.
Or let's take rasgullas, gulabjamuns, laddoos and mithais.
They are first and foremost sweets, Madame
But some, like my mother, like their sweets less-sweet;
Or like my taste-buds, who mature with age
Leaving childish chocoholism and cottage cheese cravings behind.
You may be at the political centre, Sir. I, surely, am left of centre,
But fundamental extremes only bind us in circles of continuum
And the next time you obsess, Asperger's like (note to self)
over an unironed crease or some bit of dirt,
An incomplete footnote or an excluded poet,
Unbounded optimism-pessimism, emotion-reason, kindness-firmness;
And perhaps even the next time you exercise militant
vegetarianism to spare those poor animals–
(exercise it, yes, but decide how much salt, what kind of salt)
Maybe, just maybe remember (I need to learn, but so do you)
that although salt is an extremely important ingredient in cooking,
And must certainly never be overlooked,
Salt must still be used in proportion.

ANISH VYAVAHARE

Thirsty

I am thirsty.
I drink from my salt-centered father and I gag,
I retch, I get sick, I get confined to bed.
My mother, absent like the Marathwada monsoon,
now arrives like a political promise in post-suicide haste.

This is the exact opposite of a suicide attempt though.
I slit my wrists on the blade of my father's heart
to moisten the cracked earth we grow on,
to have a better chance at losing our cactus thorns.

Life, it struggles, it survives, moves on.
The thirst isn't solved yet.
I try to drink from you, but you are a dam
that feeds many canals. The trickle you send out to me
spends itself on the journey, I suck stones
it may have touched on the way.
The stones suck me right back, crack my lips.
Once every few seasons, you drizzle on me
for an hour before you go home.
That year is a good year.

But thirst is an everyday thing,
an every hour thing.
I dowse at home, on phone,
on text, by app, in class,
by mind, with heart, in dream,
in fantasy you are a well of sweet water
and I am a pond. We slip
on the green grass that grows on
our banks, a waterfall tumbles
into our backyard,
the rain scampers like an imp,
a stream prances around
and the big sister river rushes along.

I wake up to drink a glass of water,
there is just a dreg at the bottom.
I go back to sleep, thirsty,
willing no nightmares of eating sand.

MADHU RAGHAVENDRA

Togetherness

The morning melts like ice lollies;
Faiz paints on the ceiling:
Yaha se shahar dekho;
Neruda coils up like malli poo
next to the bedside lamp
and performs 'ode to her scent'.
We have rounds of masala tea.

Later, Jack Kerouac plays on YouTube
as I mince the cabbage and peel the garlic.
I take you on a beatnik road trip, starting with
Howl, leaning by the kitchen sink, 'I saw the
best minds of my generation', and tell you
like Jack, my dad too has liver cirrhosis,
though in his case, poetry wasn't the cause.

You ask, 'How did their friendship end?'
A skeletal breeze drops by like a
long-lost friend knocking on the door.
A brown skin colours my leftover tea.
The narrow lanes lament the lack of stray dogs.
My tongue awaits the taste of taler bora
from the sweet shop opposite Ujjayanta Palace

AEKTA KHUBCHANDANI

jam spread

try the blend of orange with chocolate, coffee with banana, muskmelon and papaya, red grapes and pomegranate, kiwi and strawberries, sweet lime and pineapple, hands and toes, neck and teeth, lips with ears, head and thigh, soft nibbles on the collar bone, belly button and butter fingers, nose and nose, tongue with tongue,

love wears bindi and boots together, can dance to shakira on her pms days. we make chai with elaichi, sauf and cinnamon. we eat the pound cake two days after it's baked. 'tastes better this way', she says. she places her feet on my lap, her soft toes soak the skin on my thighs and hands. who said waves can't be manmade? i comb her hair with my finger tips.

we lie in bed, kiss each other's hand turn by turn. we're monotony at our best. *love* wears long yellow socks, an antique leather strapped watch and smiles at me with his bunny teeth. he places his palm across my waist. we slow dance to the kitchen floor, in aprons, lick our fingers after dipping them in jam jars. we're clean hands and messy mouths. we're two tongues, wide smiles and two bodies melting to one. we're closed eyes and wonder, we're cranberries with banana, we're two types of sweet, soft nibbles on the collar bone, he paints my skin with fingertips, we're belly buttons and butter fingers, nose and nose, tongue with tongue, *love* with *love*, *love* and *love*.

GITI CHANDRA

Simple Rhymes for Difficult Times
Dadri, 2015

Peace be in your streets
Let no neighbour inspect
Your larder for its meats.
Let no man suspect
Your daughter of eyeing
Mates of other castes.
Peace be in your markets
As people shop between fasts.
May those who consider dyeing
Their cloths in other hues
Choose wisely amongst colours
While paying holy dues.
Peace be in your homes
Where reading stops at sundown
When hiding certain tomes
Means riding until run down.
Let no man be left slumped
On his doorstep, stained.
Let huddles of good folk disperse
Their blood lust undrained.

Let sunsets carry what reds
We need to light our days
And nations wave what flags
They must, and go their separate ways.

Peace be upon this city
That none need earn their pity.

HIBA AHMED

The Last Supper

Has the security been beefed up now?
They enquired 'bout the scene and how.
Last time we saw one was chopped, one roasted alive
The salad bowl country seemed to be on a drive
Of unpalatable crimes
And distasteful transgressions;
They attempted to present
their humble confessions-
Shut up, you pork-mouthed jerk
Oh, pork?
No pork in my religion, d'ya hear?
No beef in mine, mister.
And in mine, no beer!
What's up with these religions of food, Sir?
To these screaming screens will you remain glued, Sir?
Shh! There's luscious violence and mouth-watering scenes of gory blood.
You may find these unappetising, I'd say it's an acquired taste.
Like caviar, it needs time, can't be digested in haste.
We've had plenty and there's a new delicacy each day!
To this inedible vigilantism, is this what you've gotta say?

I said Shh, not a word will you utter.
Just gulp down the mud,
With some sweet peanut butter.
Sir, I need answers, I'm hungry!
Ya expect me to give ya everything on a plate dear?
I am a respectable citizen- no criticism will I hear!
There's something fishy I smell, Sir,
Perhaps a funeral pyre.
Oh, it's nothin'- just some smoke without a fire!

JAGARI MUKHERJEE

Tah-dig

1

I still cook rice in open pots,
letting the fragrance that you loved
stray through the wind.
You preferred my white rice
to your Persian tah-dig,
(which
I, an adept cook, adorned for you
with red sour zereshk berries,
while we bit into the crisp oil-fried layer
at the bottom like a cake).

2

I went last year
to the best Parsee restaurant in Mumbai,
Mother and Father in tow.
I was startled to see tah-dig
on the table after ten long years.
"This is delicious," my parents exclaimed.

I remained silent, not telling them
that they had just paid Rs 700
for a dish that their daughter
could cook way better at home.

Except, it is not the same home
that I shared with you.

*Tah-dig: Rice cooked in Persian style
*Zereshk: Dried barberry fruit

MRINALINI HARCHANDRAI

Making Cheese

Laughing cows graze
bucolic joy by design
cheddaring the cud,
a pastoral mascarpone
on the label
and it all looks gouda.

Open the box
and her udder falls
out, she camemberts
the emmental details:
the fist forced its whey
into her womb
and when they threw
the babybel from the milk
bucket, she feta-ed in grief,
stilton, they mongered him
to the handbag industry,
her roquefort heart
dripped out.

She bries day
and night, mozzarella

instincts curdling
from processed separation
anxiety and hormone
concoctions too gorgonzola
to fromage, her veins bleu
from emptied breast syndrome.

Soul scarmoza darkness
edams her existence
she swisses and trembles
on the production line
slavery so gruyere
she loses comté
of her labours
on ricotta leg textures
she's aged and moulded
into crumbs.

The munsters wait
clutching toast.

But we won't rennet in
and the wheel of parmesan
keeps the raclette turning
because fondue.

SANJUKTA DAS BHOWMICK

Lost in the Aroma

That afternoon when you wandered around town

In search of that smell that drifted this way and that, making you its slave

Did you finally find the aroma?

Or was that the day when you stumbled onto me... mistaking my scent with that of the heady perfume of a half formed tiramisu?

Did you try to trace the remnants of the pattern that the chocolate made on the plate when you ran your fingers through my curls?

When you lost your way amidst the old lanes of the half-forgotten town

Did you see those wrinkled hands tirelessly kneading flour to be made into bread?

Or did you chance upon that butcher who had a special knack for slicing open the pork belly?

Did you see the pattern the blood made upon the floor as it dripped down ever so slowly from the forsaken carcass?

Did you happen to pass by that really ancient shop where they sell coloured ice lollies?

The magic of colours–red, green, pink; didn't they blind you? Did you try them or were you too afraid that they will remind you of your father buying you ice lollies in those hot summer days when nothing was enough...

Do you still follow the birds, as they make their way home, when the sky turns crimson first, and then it slowly subsides into a calm shade of purple?

How have the years changed you, subsided that frenzied madness that you once were so proud of? Now you feel no qualms about blending in with the sea of faces at the crossing of Nandan.

You no longer chase after the dying rays of the sun, you do not visit the ghats anymore in search of peace. You do not talk at length, or burst into laughter in the middle of the road.

Do you still follow the sound of the candyman going home after his day's labour? Or does the sound of his bell hurt you into remembrance of that lover you lost over a stupid fight?

That café that you visited in Harrington street still hosts brunch, that person you used to kiss still haunts the place...but do you ever trace your steps back onto its wooden stairs and relive those bygone days?

Or you skirt your way this way and that, avoiding old lovers, till you find me, waiting in some strange corner, with a book in my hand and the half worn flowers in another.

NEHA RAGHANI

An Ode to Kanda Poha

'Behold! The arrival of the king of snacks,'
announce,
the pop of mustard seeds,
the crackle of curry leaves,
and the dance of frying green chillies.
Onions turn pink
in a ghunghat of oil,
like a bride-to-be.
Bathed in wink-inducing lemon,
clothed in iodised salt,
embellished with turmeric,
and coronated with
a healthy helping of freshly chopped coriander.
Bright, fresh, yellow,
you sit on the table,
like a sun with lemon rays.

The air thick
with a citrusy smell,
you attract people,
from near and far in the house.
No invitation required.

Taste buds awakening,
heart blossoming,
you are spring on a plate.
You are a long hug
on a night of longing.
You are a peaceful siesta,
on a busy day at the office.

Oh, kanda poha!
In a world full of
dapper-looking, Instagram-worthy dishes,
you are a recluse's best friend.

ATAR HADARI

Cannibals

We were sitting around after a show
eating Nancy's chocolate Tony before it melts
and wondering if we'd ever seen
a worse Romeo kiss a worse Juliet.

She said "Who ate his head?"
I said "Sorry," and licked my thumb.
She came back with a carving set
to cut the base and podium

frozen milk chocolate milky white
off his body, which was perfectly formed
though lacking somewhat in hard facts.
I said "are you leaving some?"

I ate his buttocks too eventually,
"Well, take his buttocks too," she said.
I bit his legs. All hard. I had to put him in
one side of my mouth and bite. He was difficult.

"I've licked the buttocks
I better get beyond the thighs,"

she said. She laughed and I held her back.
Eventually we split his smile

and met in the middle of his ass
with a chocolate kiss.
Somebody nibbled on the crease
I forget now who. We tumbled into sheets

dreaming about Juliet and all that gas
under the balcony and blood and fears
alight all night on party roofs
where people were in love and felt their shivs.

ANUSREE GANGULY

Rice
Scientific Name: Oryza

O-allure! O-ardor! O-bene!
The crows caw for it, the mynah stops by.
At breaks, at end of the day.
What are you, Enticement?
More than a lost ship's homing prow,
or tantalizing Sim Sim's door!

SHRUTI SAREEN

Making Love Through Food

Conveying love through serving food
offerings upon heaped offerings, platefuls
is common in a culture which shies away
from expressing love in other ways.
Taste also as a marker of love is a common
motif in poetry. Tasting tea together,
wine together, cooking together, tasting
the beloved's lips, nose, skin, eating
the desired one. Only, I make love
to you differently. Making love in absentia.
I try to connect with you whom I yearn for
by connecting with your culture.
Axomiya food. In my case, Axomiya everything.
But this poem is about food.
The mashed aloo pitika. The bamboo shoots I love.
Dried. Or pickled. Or fried. Bamboo shoots are bamboo shoots.
The khobong raspberry tea. So many myriad teas.
The laishak. I haven't tasted the other
green leafies. The temul paan which burned my throat,
I had so much of it. The big bright yellow nemus.
The brown Kumool chawal which swells in water.
The curd with rice flakes and jaggery. The payesh.

And sweet rice pithas. Narikol laru. The tangy dal
with the ou tenga in it. Did you grow up eating these?
You wrote poetry and prose about consuming home
through food. I want to eat all of that.
I have very limited experience. I would not, however,
Have the maasor tenga, the duck, the pork, the bacon:
Forever a divide between you and me. How does he make
love to you, not knowing how these feel and taste
on your tongue. He has never eaten these either, he never will.
How does he make love to you, not knowing that?
In absentia, I eat the bhogali chowmein (like I ate
with you once, remember? Aloo paranthas, popcorn,
chowmein – not axomiya). I try to adopt Axom land.
I try to eat and dream my way back to you.

SMEETHA BHOUMIK

Magic of Flour

Make your world go 'round - Strawberry Revolving Rising Cake

Ingredients:
1 whole-wheat week,
1 carton milk of kindness,
5 ounces of soft well-chosen words (no flattery),
6 eggs from contended hens (or a page from PG Wodehouse),
6 slices of ginger, dry wit, lemongrass,
6 heaped spoonsful of sweetness, of good friendships (no added sugar),
250 gm of fresh, hopeful strawberries,
2 twists of tangy fresh lime and sarcasm,
A pinch of creative yeast,
Few drops of 'equal-rights' essence,
Few dottings of crushed desperation,
A garnish of disaster,
A hint of heartbreak,
Sprinkled with rose, dew, dawn and hope....
Beat the eggs until frothy

Add milk, all the words, and keep stirring for a while until consistent
Add the week in slowly, stirring until well balanced
Mix in all the ingredients with adoration, stir well
Place in an oven made of resilient love, stainless humour and reinforced hope

Bake at 180 degree centigrade, occasionally peeping in without judgement, letting it rise in peace. There now, peep through the glass door! Do you see? Your world. Your piece of cake.

Garnish with laughter & old song, serve hot or chilled, as the season demands.

Preserve all ingredients in thick-walled, lidded jars (like the ones grandmom had). Be careful with the despair, desperation and heartbreak, they tend to evaporate with time (use them fresh, or if unavailable, substitute with a pinch of common salt). Creativity and kindness are best preserved with practice, store in open jars every day, keep them aired. Same applies to words. Eggs should be fresh; however, the Wodehouse replacement may be old and well-thumbed. Friendships require sunlight, space and understanding (a note of caution here - sometimes you need to walk away too, in order to be able to come back, with love; don't worry, you'll get it once you start baking). The equality essence you must store within you, in every cell and fibre. The more you use, the more you will generate. Sarcasm needs no special care, it stays well in all climes. Be sparse with it. Keep the whole-wheat week fresh and nimble, jogging and happy thoughts help.

MOINAK DUTTA

Memories of a gourmet

Watching how she prepared *paturi*
Was itself a matter of great joy,
Savoring it later
Was perhaps only an extension of that happiness,
The way she marinated fish fillets,
Touching each of them with a lot of care,
Sprinkling just the amount needed of chili, coriander
flakes, pepper, ginger and garlic paste,
Mustard oil and poppy grains,
I would look at those fillets getting oily and colouring,
Smelling delicious,
Glistening too,

Then she would put them with all of her feminine care
Into banana leaves,
Her fingers with deft ease
Packing those fillets into little leafy boxes,
She would seal them using flour paste,
I would look at her practiced élan,
And admire her more,

Her fingers which worked so beautifully,

Her face which would always have a sense of bliss while she would be at the kitchen,
Her apron with floral embroidery having patches of yellow, green, red,
The smell of turmeric, chili flakes, cardamom seeds, coming from her hair,
I would admire all of them.

LINDA ASHOK

Woman on a Quest for a Perfectly Round Roti Smeared with Oil & Chopped Onions

Sometimes, I wonder
how ma in her twenties
rocked her life swinging

from one end
    of the mountain
        to the other...

She rocked it when baba
brought home his second wife

She rocked it when the roof
    refused to hold all the rain

She rocked it when she ran
    into an early menopause

as if she was ready to give
    luck her broken address

In her twenties, she rocked life
    like natural calamities
        were only her business

Except in those evenings
when the rotis wouldn't make
        a perfect circle

the basket empty of onions
and the bottle of cooking oil
just enough to give her newborn
        a massage the next day

    She would drop a tear
but get to the job nonetheless

SUDEEP SEN

Indian Dessert

Clumps of smoke simmer in the pan, and slowly
   lift to caress the outline of your breasts

as you cook, stirring spices in carrot, milk,
   and cream—ingredients that conjure

recipes of hunger and passion. As you stroke
   sugar and butter and gently melt

flakes of grated almond-shavings,
   more clumps of perfumed smoke permeate through

the silk of your shirt—now transparent in heat—
   painting the outer circle of the nipples

to a hardened edge, tasting the sweet
   skin, the surface of the crinkled base,

to a creamed mouthful of untampered delicacy.

NADEEM RAJ

Beans on Toast

I make myself coffee
And beans on toast
On a Sunday evening
You say you don't like rain
The kitchen window is teary-eyed
The wailing of drops as loud
As your absence
The fridge as empty as
The bedroom
Devoid
Of flavour
And freshness
You are time zones away
So far that the rain can't touch you
The coffee is poor comfort
The beans near expiry
The sun will be on holiday for months
I used to be able to like the rain
When indoors
Now I want to be sun kissed
The phone rings
The rain lessens for a while

LINDA JUMMAI MUSTAFA

The Big Watermelon

Have you seen the big watermelon?
Have you eaten the melon with greenish skin, red eyes and black pupils?
Have you sucked the watery juice that never fails to confuse your taste buds?
Or have you ever carried the watermelon like you carry your own baby,
Caressing it, stroking it and telling it that you love the mother melon of all melons?
The mulchy melon attacks my entrails with a tender force of love,
Nourishing my body and my soul.
The big watermelon never minds how ugly it may look,
Yet the green corrugated stripes tell you more stories about its healthy body.
Some grow their watermelon into square shapes; others, the traditional round balls;
Whatever its shape, the watermelon melts the hearts of many horrid foes,
From the times of Alexander the Great, to the great industrialisation of the new country.

The water melon is loyal to no one but the eater's sharp teeth,
And not even diamond rings which are a girl's best friend can compare
To a light snack of the water melon, to the sweet savoury feel of the water melon,
Neither can the most expensive coffee ruffle away giant balls of watermelons.

Can the watermelon love?
Can the watermelon walk?
Can the watermelon work and make money?
Can the watermelon cause a Karl Marx kind of revolution and kick the rich out of their oblivion?
China says yes; America say likely; Africa shatters quests to hold Tudor's meetings,
And makes Aphrodite jealous of Medusa and her eyes which turn everyone and everything
To stony statues and stone beasts,
Whose beliefs of a passionate love affair with Venus,
Erupts into the castration of Achilles,
All for the quiet, giant watermelon that sits majestically by the king of rumblings!
Ahoy! Says the bearded captain, whose love for the sea,
Suppresses the nostalgic ambience of the greying watermelon,
Left crying down in the ship's pantry,
The big watermelon worries no maid, no master,
Its size, its shape, and its colour corrupt the executioner's sword.

SRIVIDYA SIVAKUMAR

Sine wave Sultana

There are many things you can eat from a lover.
The first fries on a date. Popcorn that you fingerwrestle for.
Mousse with two spoons.
Sometimes he leaves a suggestive peach in your desire path.
That goodnight kiss is champagne and desperation.
When you finally breakfast together, the pancakes are piled low on a Limoges plate.
A thimbleful of maple syrup, cream and fruit.
Makaibari for him. Blue Tokai for you.
As you trace your fingers on him, eyes closed, he is food porn.
His shoulders are warm cinnamon.
His lips the chocolate cake you baked for him.
His back is a field of cocoa.
His hands are anointed with sweet coconut water.
His nipples are sugared almonds.
His cock tastes of you.
Time is cornucopia, a smorgasbord of spices and sweet sin.

There are no movie dates now. The caramel popcorn is sticky with disuse.
You drink soup for your hoarse throat and headache. He eats his appam with beef and finds the restaurant fascinating.
Dessert for one. An uninspiring butterscotch.

Your neck was once warm honey. You're breaking into hives.
Your breasts were salted caramel. It's been taken too far.
Your feet were peppermint. The herbarium is unwatered.
Your mouth tastes bitter. The food, ash. The tea is dust.
The basket of fruit is adornment.
The rum, just molasses.
Gone to seed.

URNA BOSE

Sadness Café

Shards of recollection today fill my head.
Bits of broken glass – bright, sharp, red.
Memories don't always have a happy, sepia haze.
Why, some can even set your mind ablaze.
Fuzzy, warm, cosy? No, sometimes they aren't those.
Bleak, slippery alleyways, your mind takes a turn and goes.
So, you saunter down memory lane, with your purple handbag.
You revisit a memory or two that made your spirit sag.
You sit at Sadness Café, and wonder why sadness is so sad.
You question whether it left you with something, you hadn't had.
"Bon appétit! Your dish has bitterness sprinkled there and here.
 But not all things are easy to stomach," the waiter makes it clear.
So, you take a spoonful of memory that makes you look back.
Analyse exactly where, and how deep was the crack.
Soon the waiter asks, "will you recommend us to others, ma'am?"
"Of course," you say. "Sadness is so real, chirpiness a sham."
Then you crack open the fortune cookie, lying on your plate.
It reads, "relish the depths of sadness dear, it's not
something to hate."

PRAGYA ANURAG

Back Home

Anxiety ridden onions
Brown, golden, pink –

Potatoes mashed,
baked beans, fork
and a knife, loaves of
bread crumbling
for breakfast.
Hills, hats; a small town in India, touristy,
blooming students sitting in lines.

– I cook in my mother's kitchen,
dhaniya, lehsun, adrak,
grinding and tasting
the smoke from neighbouring houses.

Wednesdays-
always English breakfast for dinner.
Bowls of jelly-
crimson, red, fuchsia,
sitting there patiently for someone to call
Dessert.

There's a small grace,
Almighty! Amen.
Strange food it seems, my school
Set in 1836, very English,
very Hogwarts like we think.

Sausages, eggs
poached and boiled,
paneer bhujiya on the side
bubbles bursting on the rim
Of the freshly brewed porridge bowls,
remembering hari chatni and achaar I savoured at home.

Cookies for evening break,
Tea/ Bournvita brown in aluminium jug.
No kettle?
Tea- barely tea.

On special days-
There's bread and chicken,
Gleaming eyes and broader smiles,
"Dal, no gravy"
The bearers said.
" 'Tis hardly a surprise,
We're no English, food
not suit stomach-
not after independence."
After dinner there's
pudding, pie and truffle.

We are not served aloo parathas,
Except on Sundays when,
a small revolt breaks out
in the small town kitchen,
that evening we are served,
Tea and samosas...
Ah! Samosa aur chai.

SHANTA ACHARYA

Taste of Childhood

My tongue never forgot the taste of childhood –

the piquancy of pineapple, subtle flavours of jackfruit,
burst of honey in sugar palm, date, lychee and starfruit,

tangy zest of tamarind, sweet aftertaste of sour amla,
bitter neem and karela, the astringent bite of jamun –

the tree-climbing, limb-bruising days of magic
plucking guava, papaya, sapetta, chasing butterflies

in the sprawl of grandfather's grove that hugged the river
bustling with wild life and islands quivering

with its siege of herons practising their moves
while we spent orgasmic summer afternoons sucking

mangoes, munching raisins, almonds and cashews,
waiting for a flash of kingfisher's indigo blue,

sipping nectar, sugarcane juice spiced with ginger,
when the world in your reach was for your pleasure,

and ghar, not bricks and mortar but a state of belonging,
Vilayat, the vast unknown out there, beckoning –

you a sapling born to stay put in the shade
of ancient banyan trees, not travel hopefully.

Who would've thought the sparkling laughter
of pomegranates would reduce you to tears,

and the ceremony of cracking open the hard exterior
carry you home to the tenderness of kernel in the belly

of coconuts, the soft, scented pulp of ripe wood apples,
the tree born from the sweat of a goddess,

its sacred leaves offered in worship, transport you
to the inner sanctum of temples?

Like oranges, apples, bananas and grapes you make
a home of the world, holding your worlds together –

the place of your birth where all your efforts to escape
landed you in a place where all your attempts to belong

always point to a world elsewhere, leaving
you in-between, in the not-this-not-that state of being,

double helix of past and future wrapped round each other,
dancing to the eternal music of the present.

This persistence of memory is no ordinary thing –
a lifeline like mother's milk, la dolce vita homecoming.

SHAMAYITA SEN

Ghore Phera: My Homecoming

I was home this winter vacation.

Kolkata isn't too cold, unlike Delhi or New York;
Just mild and welcoming enough to peel the afternoon sun off the oranges,
Juiced to perfection for a child's taste buds.

"What is home?" I asked Baba as a child,
I know he was born here, in Kolkata,
But his family comes from Dhaka.
He told me stories of Partition violence that
He had heard from his father,
While he mixed moong dal with fish bones
Into his steaming hot plate of rice,
And casually placed a soft little mold of the mixture into my mouth.
He added,
"Home is where the heart is."

While doing PK's MPhil course on "Long Migration,"
We had discussed and debated on the concept of Home.
And while I teach Home as a concept

To young adult minds now,
We see struggle and food served on the same page.

In Delhi, while sitting over a plate of mashed potato,
And tenderloin steak,
Surrounded by friends, equally home sick,
I crave home in alu-sedho-makha-ghee-bhaat.
That is comfort food, soothing my half baked Bengali soul
Living a thousand miles away from childhood delicacies of
Peas kachori and slow cooked
Mutton kosha.

Despite having lived away from Kolkata for a decade,
The homecoming lunch is what both Maa and I look forward to.
She diligently asks over the phone,
A day prior,
"What would you like to have?"

And

My mind races from
Prawn malai curry to rabri,
From mustard hilsa to mishti doi,
Liquid jaggery,
Pitha -
Everything that fine dining with friends cannot suffice,
Everything that the heart craves for.

And I shout out with excitement:
"Anything you wish to cook, Maa!
Anything that would remind me of
My cocooned childhood."

KIRITI SENGUPTA

Masala Muri

Ginger slices do not titillate
my taste-buds again.

The tangy golden of mustard oil
does not tease my nostrils anymore.

Onions fail to dew my eyes now;
they were never kept in cold water
before *Baba* chopped them; while he got
his lenses damp, *Ma* had tears.

On every stormy Sunday
we invariably had power cuts,
and *Baba* cooked dinner for
us all:

a moderate serving of *Muri* mixed with
onion, ginger and blobs of oil.

On such occasions we used to sit close,
facing each other we shared our stories;
from airing endless grievances on our barren

curriculum, the dialogues on the utility
of learning Sanskrit,
to refuting *Ma*'s advice on being courteous
even to strangers we would meet.

Our room shined in kerosene lamps!

Load-shedding no longer casts its spell;
the back-ups are prompt and steady
we order food...the mobile app comes handy,
but *Muri* seldom makes it to our monthly grocery.

The next monsoon I wish to buy
a new lantern,
and I'll light it once in a while
to accompany the old snack
and fresh stories in our family.

**Muri* is a traditional Bengali snack, otherwise called puffed rice.

ANISH VYAVAHARE

Soft Cheese

It is not hard, it is difficult,
the crust that forms on cheese
left out of its wrapper,
solid and stringy
like the exteriors of sons
left out of the hugs of their mothers.
Like anomalous water under ice
they are still soft cheese
on the inside,
softened yet in the kiln of breath,
they melt under lovers
and inside hot omelettes,
they add flavour and heft.
They get intense with age, are nibbled
on less and sometimes
in stealth, they are good
for your bones, but bad for your heart,
cheese left open in the fridge smells
of the fridge and then you
have to scrape off the top,
and now look what you have done!
You have wasted one half.

RUSHATI MUKHERJEE

Emelia

Take me to that apple tree
Where the winter sun once shone.

I can see it now through the fractured light in the far corner of the garden
Steeped in the laughter of our play.

I stack golden discs with trembling fingers
Dipped in the summer of your love.

A clean cut reveals the layers of happiness I hid
Oozing yellow upon yellow upon cream, gelled, glazed, dried
dust hugging sticky crumbs of sepia tears.

Take me to that day when the sun waltzed in your stirring eyes
and we laughed together in the echoing green
and you served us hot tea and toast
wrapped in the splendour of your love.

Fresh reels of dew, strewn through, has
The sweet running bitter running salt,
around the china vale,
in bursts of silver song
That only the glow of the here, of the now can pale,
And turn sweet once more.

Take me to those leaves

That showered in jade-glass flashes
Of poppy-perfect days I dream of
When the warmth melts across the open blue pan
And I lie still and bathe in your scent
That shimmers like the sun you once caught
and tossed some sage in
And served to me on that frosty day.

The yellows sing on my palette and grow tendrils and arms
Like eager children scrambling for love they twine and dance
Lilting taller, taller, rising monstrous out of the bowl of leaking love
Into barks into vines into trails until their seeking branches mate with the living roots in my head.

'Til I tower, my art and heart melded on that plate
Piping the tune of half-forgotten love.

It's the imperial crown of emerald shade
Netting the summer of the long-lost sun
I now hold on my head
That chased the shadows blooming on the ground
Shadows that bloom no more.

ROHINI SUNDERAM

Wine for Two

Surrounded by the debris
Of a wine for two evening
Still nibbling on Brie and breadsticks
And the honey of laughter
Scattered with nuts

Becoming friends over figs
Disagreeing
Agreeing
Teasing

Dipping strawberry memories
In chocolate sauce
Laced with whiskey

I raise another toast
Of thanks

PIESIE KOFI BABONE

Jollof Battle

Perhaps this battle will never end.
Perhaps we will all join this fight.
The chicken and the egg, who came first?
Man and woman, who came first?
Perhaps these battles will never end.
Shatta Wale and Stone Bwoy, who is the best?
And finally, the biggest of the fights:
Ghana Jollof and Nigeria Jollof, which is the best?

The chefs take note and observers get worried.
Even teachers learn as orators take the stage.
The careful combination of ingredients
Is what will make it to the event:
The heat and utensils contribute their lot as well.
The judges are silent about the results,
Confused as to which is the best.

Let all the best chefs come from both ends.
Let all the ingredients take to the stand.
Let bloggers blog and gluttons be judges.
Today be today. Everything else can wait.
Serve some palm wine while we wait.
Let's settle this battle once and for all.
Let's see if Ghana Jollof will beat Nigeria Jollof again.
Oh! This Jollof battle needs a definite end.

PARESH TIWARI

At Gol Darwaza

Like clock-work he comes, bearing pale-yellow clouds on his head. Setting down his wares, he scoops out a dollop of *makhan-malai*–a tango of milk, sugar, cardamom spattered with the first dew of morning–and flicks it into a bowl of dried leaves. The scale moves just a breath.

> Then she. Bare-foot.
> Her salwar shredded at the hem.

The muezzin's call hangs inverted on overhead wires. The buildings huddle together, blowing puffs of hot breath over the fingers of time. A lone mongrel, her tail curled between her hinds, shivers in the throes of a dream that would end at the noir walls of an empty stomach. It's early and cold. Cold enough to warrant the life of thirty-nine street dwellers last night.

> Hair matted. Tangled. Her eyes wild.
> A pair of hands claw the air behind.

Fog settles thick over windows. A murder of crows and milk vans prowl the morning. A man on a scooter slips a spoonful of *makhan* under his bushy moustache. Closes his eyes.

> The opaque stench of petrol fills the air.
> Bored heads follow the trajectory of her feet.
> Then trail to the men following her.

A car brakes. Skids, hitting the scooter.

> Her feet pound the road.
> Weaving in. Then out.
> Her heart pounds her breasts.

His hand catches up. A vice around her wrist.

the width
of a shriek...stepping over
*   a clubbed mongrel*

JENNY CURRIER

Gelato, Interrupted

A stranger startled me in Italy, saying,
"The way you are eating gelato,
I've never seen anything like it.
My friends tell me I eat slowly,
But you...you are slower even than me."
The late hour hid my blushing cheeks,
caught as I was in such a scandalous affair,
interrupted,
sensuously licking the sweet cream
from my spoon (I prefer small spoons,
so as not to indulge too quickly),
savoring the swirly folds of Panna Semifreddo,
<<cream, semi-frozen>>
dispensed at the hands of the Italian woman
who told me, "This is my specialty,"
dense whipped cream, luscious and heavenly,
a modern day manna.

The stranger looked at me
imploringly.
"You must really enjoy it."

My tongue, still tingling,
finally formed the words,
"It's the best I've ever had,"
and with a final scrape of the cup,
I sucked the small spoon clean.

SHARMILA RAY

Mangoes And Jackfruits

Will you come down and sit beside me
amidst a world of mango and jackfruit trees
 or be distant like cherry trees in far off lands?
Touch me and it is the mango pulp sweet and smooth
that I have eaten. Masses of yellow-orange make my
skin tawny.
and my flesh entwined with leaves and branches.
You will find wild flowers and mystic hour and I shall
wrap you in mango-bark and memories freezing
 inside luscious jackfruit. Smell the perfume that waltzes
from
tree to tree and then settles on the damp floor.
If only you would come the mangoes and jackfruits
would expand and touch the stars
and we would merge with the carpet of time.

GABRIEL AWUAH MAINOO

Morning Rites

At every crack of sunshine
I perform a solemn ritual:
Oh, never again
Will I die of gastric wars!

Through the balcony
The shifting sun stalks with an eye
As I part my palms
While the coffee goes up and down
And the palm drops
The bread goes up and down
And the hand drops
The cheese goes up and down
And the cheek drops
The wheat goes up and down
And my belly draws

I halt a while and dream of fruits
I naked bananas
And wash apples
I slice strawberries
And suck their blood
Oh, I shall be strong in the day
Until the pull of sundown!

TEMIDAYO OPEYEMI JACOB

My Coffee

My goodness!
My coffee was brewed
in a cup with killer-curves.
Brown skinned: like chocolates
found in the big stores in London.
Hot: like the afternoon sun found
at the upper end of the North.
Sweet: like the candies meant
for kids who love to lick their
lips with the tip of their tongues.
Rich: like a meal highly seasoned.

Every morning I love to wake up to
see my coffee on my bed, beside me,
waiting for my hands to feel
and touch the cup, before I stir it.
When I stir, I hold my coffee firmly
and stir harder, deeper, and harder.
When I stir, my coffee blows my
mind and takes my breath away.
My coffee is therapeutic. I like my
coffee dark, hot, sweet and rich.
Today
I stirred my coffee like a missionary.
Tomorrow,
I'll stir my coffee like a cute pooch.

JESS SEVETSON

Mango

Does that mango tree,
branches heavy with swollen fruits,
swaying provocatively,
writhe with anticipation of the day
when your hand reaches up,
cups a fruit,
squeezes it for ripeness,
& pulls it roughly down,
claiming it for-the-afternoon-forever?

Stripping away the colorful rind,
raising the pulp to your parted lips
& greedily sinking your teeth into its flesh
until the juices run sweetly down your chin,

does the mango wish only that you
could devour it over
and over again?

PARESH TIWARI

Lorem Ipsum

There's an apple in the shallow bowl by the window. Glistening. Crisp. Its red a peculiar shade of desire. Alive to the touch.

No one remembers how to converse with the apple anymore. It's an art lost in the garden of Eden. There's much the apple could have said. Like how a handful of plums stain your lips forever. How the seeds you spit out, grow into sculptures. And how when bitten right, a single mango births seven poems.

Each more sinful than the last.

the fragrance
of night-blooming cacti...
her buttons undone

KIRITI SENGUPTA

Time and Tide

It was 8 am and the butler inquired, *What would you like to have for your breakfast, Sir?* We partied last night with a group of young ladies. We had good food with plenty of drinks. I cautiously ordered a slice of bread and a cheese omelet. I heard the boy instructing a woman-cook. It was an open kitchen arrangement, and I saw a Bengali widow in her early forties placing the bread-slice in the toaster. She set the time and quickly picked two eggs from the basket. I noticed her bright eyes as she broke the eggs.

The boy served me breakfast on a white dish. The bread was perfect, but the omelet looked weird. I could make out the woman did not whisk the yolks properly. A bit annoyed with the quality of service, I asked the waiter, *Is she a new appointee?* He hesitantly replied, *She is my aunt, Sir. She lives in our ancestral home; she lost her husband when she was only eighteen!*

MADHU RAGHAVENDRA

Amin

Tumblers of *poka* are up in the air.
A grand old pig's grunt shakes the Basar Valley.
Three young men stand on it, calm it down,
tie its legs with bamboo strips, sharpen a bamboo,
and pierce it until it perforates the heart —
rivulets of blood runs red in celebration.
The eyes shut slowly. The mountains fade
as the pig's last huff raises a cloud of dust —
the tail wrapped in *okko* leaf,
the hair burnt with torch flame,
the skin scraped with a *dao*,
the abdomen slit smoothly,
liver and intestines pulled out,
the blood on a vessel.
The shaman studies the liver.
The omen is good!
Water in a large pot,
blood diluted,
meat minced,
rice grain mixed,
ginger grated,

garlic shredded,
salt added to taste.
Cook it to a gruel, and the *amin* is ready.
Offerings are best served warm.

---

*Amin is a kind of porridge usually prepared on special occasions in Arunachal Pradesh by adding chicken or pork or beef or Indian Gaur. Poka is a local rice wine.

ANISH VYAVAHARE

Garam Masala

I commit fraud,
I cheat,
you are not the first
I meet today, you are not
the first kiss,
not the first caress,
not the first care,
my smell hasn't changed,
you are just smelling others on me;
your side of the footpath
is slippery by wear,
the watchman by now
has an indifferent glare,
and the lighter is low on fuel
although I just bought it today.
I always give you
a new soup spoon that
hasn't tasted another mouth,
but the soup's been around,
and there is such a thing as
your towel in the house.
I haven't had time to change
the sheets, so we meet

on the granite oata
of the living room,
the easier to make fresh
after you leave,
for I commit fraud,
I cheat,
you are not the last
one I meet today,
another will lick
you on my lips,
retrace the scratch
you leave on my ribs,
but my breath, now,
smells forever of you.
Not only of you, though,
for I am a chimera,
a quilt of a person,
garam masala,
I lie when I say I cheat,
you blend in the grind, but
you are never lost in it, I pick
your flavour out each whiff,
and when the masala is
of only these many
ingredients, I can't
imagine if star anise said
it didn't want to be part
of the mix.

*garam– hot as in temperature, food that raises the temperature of the body
*masala– individual spice or spice mix or ground spice mix
*oata– platform

GITI CHANDRA

How Cooking Almost Killed the Cat

So today the cat fell out
The kitchen window. All
I want to say about
This is, it wasn't me. I
Didn't do it. The fall
Doesn't follow from the fact
That I opened it. Wide.
Or rather – wider. Why hide
The fact that a well cooked
Meal requires ventilation.
Needless to say that the family
That denies any facilitation
In the matter, needed no fervent
Invitation to the heaped platters.
I wish to also place on record
My last words to the lord
Of the manor (who flatters
Himself as innocent of the crime):
Shut the window, I clearly said
As he heaved over in his bed.
Or the cat, I swear to god,

Will fall out. He laughs now,
And thinks it's funny to point out how
This is one down out of nine.
So I'm saying this for the last
Time: this is everyone's fault
But mine.

NABANITA SENGUPTA

Nurtured Cravings

1.
She eyed her brother's shorts and shirts
then glanced at chicken legs,
juicy succulent, as they peeped
from the kitchen shelf.
Yet she knew, her tattered frock
Wouldn't measure up to them.

2.
Your throwaways piled on throwaways,
her stomach filled on these
leftover combos of gourmet,
you belched on meat and sweets.
Your lean and toned physique,
her gain in calories!

3.
Pujas followed their tithis,
her menstrual flow its own
Devi this year won't eat her bhog,
But would She bless her womb?

4.
That life within her stirred a joy
and a delicious craving.
Fruits, cookies and all those goodies
for Nine Months at her becking!
Carpe diem - was that her thoughts?
Munching on her munch-ins ...

KIRITI SENGUPTA

Clarity

I have seen my mother
preparing *ghee* out of milk—
She never used butter
to clarify it further

She'd boil and store the milk
in large quantities for days
Once cooled, she'd separate
thick layers of yellow froth—
Layer after layer she filled
the storage pot, then put it on burner,
which filled the house with aromatic milk

So organic is my memory—
The granular residue lifted us to heaven
Ah! Pious *ghee*, and incorrigible!

*Ghee is clarified butter.

LINDA ASHOK

No Love but Good Meat

The poet was sitting all idle
waiting for rain to wash the dirt
from his reading glasses
while he smoked his pen
and chewed images
of the world cooking for him
some delicious comfort

His wife opened the refrigerator
to find a lemon and two onions
and a pizza wrapped in garden fungus
What do we eat? she asked & the poet
nonchalant in his manners said,
Can we have ourselves grilled in love
with rings of onion and a dash of lemon?

SHARMILA RAY

Apple

Would you believe if I say that an Apple can actually speak?
It nestled in my palm russet and solid talking of pink apple blossoms,
 leaves, green-opal, serrated with downy undersides. Its juices dripping
and fingers grew out of it and caressed me. I carried it to
my mind-spot wrapped in warmth and love. A sort of life sailing you can say.

The apple shriveled, like eyes squinting to see the distant past.
The aroma of wild steppes of Central Asia engulfed my nostrils.
 The apple whispered that it was here that the first form was formed
 and then it's voyage across oceans and continents, its core corroded by elements.
Sounds fantastic isn't it?

But believe me anything can speak like a tear housing nostalgia,
grandmother's chair or the birth of earth in half-bloomed buds.

KABIR DAS

Couplets
Translated from Hindustani by Somrita Urni Ganguly

I shan't come, nor shall I go.
I shan't live, nor shall I die.

I'll chant my lord's name like a mantra
And lose myself in that prayer.

I am a bowl, and the plate.
I am Man, and Woman.

I am a wood apple, I am a sweet lime.
I am a Muslim, I am a Hindu.

I am fish, and my own fishing-net,
I am the fisherman, and I am Time.

I am Kabir, yet I am no one/ nothing.
I am neither dead, nor am I alive.

SUDEEP SEN

Eating Rice & Fish

1.

Delicately sheathed,
   wrapped
in papery husk—

I love the feel and
   elegance of long slender
rice grains—

their seduction
   and charm,
their aroma and shape—

their fine flavour
   and
the deep virgin taste.

2.

I use my finger-tips
   to pry open,

feel, and sense

the hidden taste
　of fish—
its flesh and scales,

its coarseness
　and gloss,
its geometry,

its muscle-bone
　and tone—
Gently, I relish it all.

Notes on the Editor

Somrita Urni Ganguly is a professor, poet, and literary translator, soon to complete her PhD from Jawaharlal Nehru University, New Delhi. She was affiliated with Brown University, Rhode Island, as a Fulbright doctoral research fellow (2018 - 2019) and has taught British Literature to undergraduate students in Delhi and Calcutta. She translates from Bengali and Hindi to English and was selected by the National Centre for Writing, UK, as an emerging translator in 2016. She was invited as translator-in-residence at Cove Park, Scotland, in October 2017, and in December 2017 she was invited as poet-in-residence at Arcs of a Circle, Mumbai, an artistes' residency organized by the US Consulate in Bombay. Somrita's work has been showcased at the 2017 London Book Fair and she has been published by Juggernaut Books, BEE Books, and Seagull Books, and in *Asymptote*, *Words Without Borders*, *In Other Words*, and *Muse India*, among others.

Somrita has presented research papers at various national and international conferences in India, Singapore, UK, and USA. She has thirteen academic publications to her credit, and is a recipient of the Jawaharlal Nehru Memorial Fund Award (2013) and the Sarojini Dutta Memorial Prize (2011).

Somrita has recently completed translating a political biography, an anthology of lyrical verses by Shankarlal Sengupta, a five-volume novel-in-verse by Purnendu Pattrea, a contemporary re-telling of *The Mahabharata*, and Dinesh Chandra Chattopadhyay's novel *Firesongs*. She is presently translating a novel by Rabindranath Tagore, and a film script by Satyajit Ray.

Notes on the Contributors

Aekta Khubchandani is a writer and poet who believes that everything is temporary. Today, she wants to be a cat-lady with a wand that grows flowers. Her work has been featured in *The Aerogram, Narrow Road, The Bangalore Review, Warehouse Zine,* and *Quail Bell Magazine* among others. Her work has also been published in print in the anthology *Equiverse Space* by WE, *Best of Mad Swirl: 2018,* and *Map called Home* by Kitaab. Her fiction and poetry entries have been long-listed twice for Toto Awards (2018, 2019) for Creative Writing in English by TFA. Her spoken word poetry has travelled in India and to Bhutan. She is the winner of the English slam at Arcs-of-a-circle Artists' Residency's event moderated by Rochelle Potkar. She secured the first place in Mumbai Regional Qualifier and the second place in the National Slam at Waves fest conducted by BITS Pilani Goa, in 2018.

Ana Gardner is the errant daughter of several generations of physicists and engineers, who fell in love with words instead of numbers. Thus, they exiled her across the ocean. She currently resides in southern Massachusetts with her partner and more pets than strictly advisable, though she hails from a small town in the Balkans called Breza. She spends her free time disastrously failing to recreate family recipes with western ingredients. Her work has appeared in *The Dime Show Review, Animal Literary Magazine*, and others, and is upcoming in *The Colored Lens*.

Anish Vyavahare eats and cooks food. He has no idea of what is real and what is maya, and whether any of it really matters. He is currently in search of all that man has searched for, for millennia: clean air, clean water, chemical-free food, and silence. His immediate aspiration is to be bread-cheese-alcohol independent from industrial society.

Anusree Ganguly is a poet who has penned for *Sahitya Akademi's Indian Literature, The Statesman*'s Festival Issue, the Poetry Society of India's *The Journal* and elsewhere. She likes to write essays too on groundbreaking thoughts which inspire and motivate others to live and think along with them. She also likes to read Jane Austen, Charlotte Bronte, Adrienne Rich, and Toni Morrison because she thinks they make not only great writers/ poets but also great artisans creating images that hit the readers with their arrows of truth. Anusree hopes one day to find an equally rewarding image that will woo her as much as it will her readers. She is an editor of the English language by profession and an alumna of Jadavpur University.

Ardra Manasi is a published poet in Malayalam and English. Born and raised in Kerala, South India, she is a development practitioner and writer based in New York City and has served as a former policy consultant with the United Nations. Her writings [poetry and prose] have appeared in *Reading Hour, Parentheses Journal, Silk and Smoke, Sahitya Akademi's Indian Literature* [forthcoming], *The News Minute, Huffington Post, Madras Courier* and elsewhere. On Twitter, she is @ArdraManasi.

Atar Hadari's *Songs from Bialik: Selected Poems of H. N. Bialik* (Syracuse University Press) was a finalist for the American Literary Translators' Association award and his debut collection, *Rembrandt's Bible*, was published by Indigo Dreams in 2013. *Lives of the Dead: Poems of Hanoch Levin* won a Pen Translates award and is out now from Arc Publications. He contributes a monthly verse bible translation column to MOSAIC magazine and is currently a Vice-Chancellor's PhD Scholar in Theology at Liverpool Hope University where he's writing on William Tyndale's translation of *Deuteronomy* and the way it was edited to become the *King James Version*.

Chandramohan S is an Indian English Dalit poet and literary critic based in Trivandrum, Kerala. He is part of the P.K. Rosi Foundation, a cultural collective (named after the legendary, pioneering Dalit actress) that seeks to de-marginalize Dalit-Bahujans. His poems were shortlisted for the Srinivas Rayaprol Poetry Prize 2016. His second collection of poems, titled *Letters to Namdeo Dhasal*, was a runner up at M Harish Govind Poetry Prize, Poetry Chain, Trivandrum. He was instrumental in organizing literary meets of English poets of Kerala for the Ayyappa Panicker Foundation and was a resident at the International Writing Program (IWP-2018) at the University of Iowa.

Cristina Peri Rossi is a Uruguayan novelist, poet, and translator. Born in Montevideo, she has lived in Barcelona since the 1970s when she went into political exile. Peri Rossi has published nineteen books of poetry, earning her many literary prizes in the genre including the Rafael Alberti International Poetry Prize, the City of Torrevieja International Poetry Prize, and the Loewe Foundation International Poetry Prize.

Elizabeth Rose is in love with the impossibility of recreating meaning and sound across languages. She translates from Spanish and German into English and researches the intersections of translation, exile, and queer perspectives in literature. She received her MA from the University of Illinois in Translation Studies. Her work has appeared in *Alchemy, Tupelo Quarterly* and *Raspa Magazine*.

Felix Green is a German-Australian poet and translator from Hahndorf, South Australia. He has published poems and translations in France, the UK, the US, Australia, and Mexico. He currently lives in Providence, Rhode Island, where he has just completed his PhD in Comparative Literature at Brown University.

Gabriel Awuah Mainoo, author of *Travellers Gather Dust and Lust*, is a Ghanaian award-winning writer, a tennis professional, lyricist and playwright studying at the University of Cape Coast. His poem 'Taunt' won best satire of the year 2017 on Voices of African poets. He serves as project manager to the Ghana Writes literary group and creative editor to Writers Global Movement magazine. Mainoo is an internationally anthologized poet who has featured on *Writers Space Africa*, the Ghana Writes journal, *Hennens Observer, Kalahari Review, Haiku Universe Journal,* and elsewhere. He is a contributor to Best New African Poets 2018, and *Bodies & Scars* anthology, among others.

Giti Chandra is currently Senior Researcher and Lecturer with the United Nations University in Reykjavik, and has been Associate Professor, Dept. of English, at St. Stephen's College, Delhi. Along with some short stories and poems, her fantasy series, *The Book of Guardians Trilogy*, is now complete, with the last of the series, *The Eye of the Archer*, expected to be out soon; the first two books are *The Fang of Summoning* (Hachette: 2010), and

The Bones of Stars (Hachette: 2013). Sadly, nobody cares about her first non-fiction book, a groundbreaking academic work on violence, but the next two - on the global #MeToo movement, and on public discourses of colonial violence - are definitely going to be bestsellers. Giti writes poetry in April, paints on Wednesdays, has a PhD from Rutgers, and feels that people would do well to learn that a cello is not an oversized violin. She lives in Reykjavik with a husband, two kids, a dog, and a cat.

Prof. **GJV Prasad** discusses life and literature at Jawaharlal Nehru University, New Delhi, where he is Professor of English. His major research interests are Contemporary Theatre, Indian English Literature, Dalit Writings, Australian Literature, and Translation Theory, and he has published extensively in these areas. He is also a poet, novelist and translator. His novel *A Clean Breast* was shortlisted for the Commonwealth Prize for best first book from the Eurasia region in 1994. He is the current Chairperson of the Indian Association for Commonwealth Literature and Language Studies.

Hiba Ahmed is a research scholar at the University of Delhi and is working on the politics of the Indian Muslim's identity in contemporary India and a post-truth environment. Along with her research, she is currently teaching at Zakir Hussain Delhi College. She did her post-graduation from Jawaharlal Nehru University and that is where most of her own politics was shaped. Creative writing is her escape from the ordeal that academia often turns into; writing poetry offers her solace. She believes that turning into a creative writer allows one brief moments of absolute power in an environment that renders one powerless.

Jagari Mukherjee holds an MA in English Language and Literature from the University of Pune, and was awarded a gold medal and several prizes by the University for excelling in her discipline. Her poems and other creative pieces have been published in different venues both in India and abroad. She is a Best of the Net 2018 nominee, a DAAD scholar from Technical University, Dresden, Germany, a Bear River alumna, and the winner of the Poeisis Award for Excellence in Poetry 2019, among other awards. She recently won the Reuel International Prize for Poetry 2019. Her first poetry collection entitled *Blue Rose* was published by Bhashalipi, Kolkata, and her first chapbook is forthcoming this year from Cherry-House Press, Illinois, USA. She is currently pursuing a PhD from Seacom Skills University, Bolpur, India.

Jenny Currier is a former dolphin trainer, English teacher, and desert dweller, now living in Providence, Rhode Island. She is *Motif Magazine*'s food editor and writer, RI food tour's cultural ambassador, blogger, author and world traveler. Her work has been published online in *Wanderlust* and *Vagabond* magazines and is forthcoming in *The Sunlight Press* and *The Tiger Moth Review*. She writes about taking leaps of faith, traveling, and finding joy in everyday experiences. She is working on a book set in Greece.

Jess Sevetson is an American scientist and writer from East Hartford, Connecticut. Her work has been published in a range of venues including the *Journal of Neurophysiology*, Technology Networks, and *Catalyst*. She lives in Providence with her cat, Rascal, and is presently completing her PhD in Neuroscience at Brown University.

Kiriti Sengupta, who has been awarded the Rabindranath Tagore Literary Prize (2018) for his contribution to literature, is a poet, editor, translator, and publisher from Calcutta. He has published ten books of poetry and prose, including *Rituals, Solitary Stillness, Reflections on Salvation, The Earthen Flute, A Freshman's Welcome, Healing Waters Floating Lamps, The Reverse Tree, My Dazzling Bards, My Glass of Wine, The Reciting Pens*, and *The Unheard I*; two books of translation, *Desirous Water* by Sumita Nandy, *Poem Continuous–Reincarnated Expressions* by Bibhas Roy Chowdhury; and he is the co-editor of five anthologies, *Scaling Heights, Jora Sanko–The Joined Bridge, Epitaphs, Sankarak*, and *Selfhood*. Sengupta's poems have been published/ accepted for publication at *The Common, Headway Quarterly, Moria Online, The Mark Literary Review*, and *Mad Swirl*, among other places. More at www.kiritisengupta.com.

Linda Ashok is a poet from India. She is the author of *whorelight* (Hawakal, 2017), runs the annual RL Poetry Award (since 2013), directs RLFPA EDITIONS (since 2018), and edits the Best Indian Poetry series (since 2018). Her poems have appeared in *Crab Orchard Review, McNeese Review, The Common, Pointed Circle*, and several others in print and online. Linda is the recipient of the 2017 Charles Wallace Fellowship by the University of Chichester, UK, & the 2018 Villa Sarkia Residency by Nuoren Voiman Liitto, Norway. More about her on www.lindaashok.com.

Madhu Raghavendra is a poet, and social development practitioner. He is the founder of Poetry Couture, one of India's largest spoken word poetry initiatives. His poetry movement has created free spaces for poetry in many cities of India. His debut book of poems, *Make Me Some Love To Eat,* has been well received nationwide, and is in its fourth edition. He has read poetry, and conducted performance poetry workshops at many schools, institutions, and literary festivals across India. He has been a part of Sahitya Akademi's Young Writers festival in Jammu. He was a resident artist at Basar Confluence, Arunachal Pradesh's first artist residency programme. He currently lives in Guwahati.

Born on September 5, 1977, **Moinak Dutta** has been writing poems and stories from his school days. He is presently engaged as a teacher of English in a government sponsored institution. Many of his poems and stories have been published in national and international anthologies and magazines and also dailies including *Madras Courier, The Statesman, World Peace* poetry anthology, *Spillwords, Setu, Riding and Writing, The Indian Periodical, Pangolin Review, Tuck Magazine, Duane's Poetree, Story Mirror, Tell me your story, Nature Writing, Oddball, Soft Cartel, Diff Truths, Ethos Literary Journal, The Literary Fairy Tales, Defiant Dreams* (a collection of stories on women empowerment published by Readomania, New Delhi), *Dynami Zois* (a selection of short stories), *Muffled Moans Unleashed* (a special anthology against women and child abuse & gender violence, published by Authorspress, New Delhi,), and others. He has written several book reviews and essays and also published two works of fiction. He blogs at www.theboatsong.blogspot.com.

Mrinalini Harchandrai is the author of *A Bombay in My Beat*, a collection of poems that explores the soundtrack of the city, personal cadences and jazz poetry. Her poem won first prize in *The Barre* (2017), and she was a finalist for the Stephen A. DiBiase Poetry Prize 2019. Her short stories have been longlisted for the Commonwealth Short Story Prize 2018 and selected as a Top Pick (2018) with Juggernaut Books, India. Her work has been anthologized in *The Brave New World of Goan Writing 2018* and RLFPA Editions' *Best Indian Poetry 2018*.

Mustafa Linda Jummai teaches English and literature-in-English at Ibrahim Babangida Badamasi University Lapai, Niger State in Nigeria. With a first degree in Mass-Communication/ English, Mustafa ventured into journalism. A teacher, journalist, novelist, poet and designer, Mustafa has written a number of poems and is one of the poets published in *The Markas*, an anthology featuring poems on the menace of Boko Haram, edited by one of Nigeria's renowned poets, Tanure Ojaide. She is currently a post graduate student at the University of Ilorin, Nigeria.

Dr. **Nabanita Sengupta** is presently working as assistant professor in English at Sarsuna College, affiliated to the University of Calcutta. Her areas of specialization are nineteenth century travel writings, women's studies, and translation studies. She has participated as translator in workshops of Sahitya Akademi, Viswa-Bharati, and others. She has presented papers in various national and international seminars in India and abroad. Recently, she was the co-convenor of an International webinar on 'Organised Higher Academics in South Asia' which brought together various universities and scholars from India and abroad using ICT and led to an interesting discourse on South Asian studies. She has co-edited a volume for *Café Dissensus* on women-displacement in South Asia. Her creative writings have also been published at various journals like *Muse India*, *Coldnoon*, *NewsMinute.in*, etc. She may be contacted at nabanita.sengupta@gmail.com.

Nadeem Raj moved from the slumbering suburbs of Udaipur to the anxious adrenalin-rush of Bombay at age 17. Though at complete odds with his personality, this is the city that feels closest to something like home because the spirit-crushing mass also provides anonymity and a chance for reinvention. Since then he has spent the better part of 14 years wandering its streets, half-fitting in. He tries to blend humor in his work to mask his cynicism and sense of dread, calling himself an unabashed romantic and gastro-poet and exploring complex themes like love, displacement and cheesecake through words. He was introduced to performance poetry a couple of years ago and has accomplished a lot in his short time on stage, becoming the first Bombay Poetry Slam winner in November 2016 and then attaining the title of the Bombay Grand Slam Champion a year later and performing at many prestigious events and venues.

Neha Raghani was born an engineer and grew up to be a spoken word poet. She is a hoarder of books, more than anything else. She was part of *The Restaurant At The End Of The Universe* spoken word poetry evening, which was the depiction of a restaurant quite unlike any other. She won the Mumbai Poetry Slam May 2017 and bagged the second prize at The Grand Slam November 2017 organised by Rochelle D'Silva. She has been a featured artist at events like Words Tell Stories, Stories in the shed, and The Blind Book Date. She was part of the first ever Poetry College batch conducted by Anish Vyavahare. She has volunteered with literary events like Jaipur Literature Festival, Kala Ghoda Arts Festival, and Arcs of A Circle artists' residency organised by Rochelle Potkar. She currently works as a content writer at a tech start-up in Mumbai.

Norbert Góra is a 29 year old poet and writer from Poland. He is the author of more than a hundred poems which have been published in poetry anthologies in USA, UK, India, Nigeria, Kenya and Australia.

Poet, artist, and editor **Paresh Tiwari** has been widely published, especially in the sub-genre of Japanese poetry. A Pushcart Prize nominee, he has published two widely acclaimed collections of poetry – *An inch of Sky* and *Raindrops chasing Raindrops*. His latest collection of haibun *Raindrops chasing Raindrops* is the recipient of the 'Touchstone Distinguished Book Awards – 2017'. His works are being used as cornerstones for close reading and creative discussions by readers across the world. He is the resident cartoonist for *Cattails*, a journal by the United Haiku and Tanka Society, USA, and the serving haibun editor of the online literary magazine *Narrow Road*, a tri-annual publication. Paresh has read his works at various literature festivals, cafés, theatres, and galleries and has conducted haibun workshops at venues across India in an attempt to dismantle the boundaries that keep the various forms of poetry and literature from sharing the same spaces. Find him on www.pareshtiwari.co.in.

Piesie Kofi Babone is an African poet, consultant, presenter, and author. He lives in Ghana and has published two poetry collections: *Hands of Gold* and *Crow in the Sky*. He observes life closely and tries to capture life's profound happenings in his write-ups. As a writer, he is confident that the best is yet to happen.

Pragya Anurag has been writing from a very early age. Her writing is reflective of her inner turmoil and grief, which find an expression in her works. A student of literature, she has completed her MA in English and is now pursuing higher education. Growing up in a missionary school, her imagination runs amidst the mountains and galleries that were a part of her childhood landscape. Her writing, on most occasions, represents raw emotion and deep empathy towards the subject. As a child, she would write novels and short stories that would get circulated amongst her friends in class. Her writing does not usually follow a linear form, instead it meanders into different directions that quench those temporary musings which emerge from a thought planting itself in the midst of the poem. She believes in equality and the freedom of choice.

Rochelle Potkar's poem 'The girl from Lal Bazaar' was shortlisted for the Gregory O' Donoghue International Poetry Prize 2018; 'To Daraza' won the 2018 Norton Girault Literary Prize in poetry; 'Place' won an honorable mention at Asian Cha's Auditory Cortex; 'Skirt' was made into a poetry film by Philippa Collie Cousins for the Visible Poetry Project; 'War Specials' won first runner-up at The Great Indian Poetry Contest 2018; and 'Amber' won a place in Hongkong's Proverse Poetry Prize 2018 anthology. As a critic, her book reviews have appeared in *Wasafiri*, *Sahitya Akademi's Indian Literature*, *Asian Cha*, and *Chandrabhaga*. *Four Degrees of Separation* and *Paper Asylum* are her books of poetry. Her upcoming poetry collection *The Inglorious Coins of the Counting House* was longlisted at the Eyewear Publishing, Beverly Prize UK.

A Canadian of Indian origin, **Rohini Sunderam** dabbles in all kinds of verse, satirical, funny, and contemplative. She has contributed to several anthologies by Robin Barratt. Her poems have been selected in international competitions for publication in *Poetry Rivals* (Remus House, UK) 2012; and *Dilliwali* (Bushra Alvi Razzak, India). Her books *Corpoetry*, *Desert Flower* and *Five Lives One Day in Bahrain* are published by Ex-L-Ence UK and available on Amazon. Her poem 'Birth Pangs' was featured in The Society of Classical Poets (May 2018), her entry in their Rhyming Riddle contest placed seventh. Her story 'Your rebirth, My death' was shortlisted in The Atlantis Short Story Contest 2013 and was published by Expanded Horizons (September 2018). She was a participant in the Colours of Life annual poetry festival in Bahrain from 2012 – 2018. She is a founder/ director of the Bahrain Writers' Circle.

Rushati Mukherjee is a journalist, blogger, translator, and poet. Her poems have been published in *The Bangalore Literary Review*; *Chaicopy*, the literary journal of Manipal Centre for Humanities; the *Curious Cosmos Zine* by Erin Hanson and Berlin Art-Parasites, and are due to be published by HarperCollins in an anthology of South Asian queer poetry. She has translated graphic novels from Bengali to English, due to be published by BEE Books. She was a campus reporter for *t2-The Telegraph* and has written for *Hindustan Times*, *The Deccan Chronicle*, and *Kindle*, the literary magazine. She has blogged for the Jaipur Literature Festival, the Apeejay Kolkata Literature Festival, and the Kolkata Literature Festival, and regularly conducts interviews of authors, poets, and activists on her blog, Spiktinot. She was selected to attend Future News Worldwide, a conference for young journalists organized by the British Council. She recently graduated from Jadavpur University with an MA in English.

Sanjukta Das Bhowmick completed her Masters in English Literature from Miranda House, Delhi University, in 2017. Her interests include reading literary fiction, non-fiction essays, graphic novels, and historical fiction. She dabbles in composing verses from time to time. She likes experimenting with different genres and painting glass bottles. She absolutely loves traveling and finds it a very good way to put her artistic skills to use. One can find her amidst the mountains at least twice a year.

Shamayita Sen is a PhD research scholar in the Department of English, University of Delhi. Her interest area in academic research lies in Indian Literature, Modernism, Political Literature and theories on the body, violence and gender. She is from Kolkata, West Bengal, India, and currently based in Delhi, India.

Shanta Acharya, born and educated in Cuttack, India, won a scholarship to Oxford, and was among the first batch of women admitted to Worcester College in 1979. A recipient of the Violet Vaughan Morgan Fellowship, she was awarded the Doctor of Philosophy for her work on Ralph Waldo Emerson. She was a Visiting Scholar in the Department of English and American Literature and Languages at Harvard University before moving to London. The author of eleven books, her latest is *Imagine: New and Selected Poems* (HarperCollins, India; 2017). Her publications range from poetry, literary criticism and fiction to finance. Her first novel, *A World Elsewhere*, was published in 2015. Her poems, articles and reviews have appeared in major publications worldwide. Founder of Poetry in the House, Shanta hosted a series of monthly poetry readings at Lauderdale House, Highgate, London, from 1996-2015. She served twice on the board of trustees of the Poetry Society in the UK.

Dr. **Sharmila Ray** is a poet and non-fiction essayist, writing in English and anthologised and featured in India and abroad. Her poems, short stories and non-fictional essays have appeared in various national and international magazines and journals. She is an Associate Professor and Head of the Department of History at City College, Kolkata. She has authored nine books of poetry. She was on the English Board of Sahitya Akademi. She conducted poetry workshops organized by the British Council, Poetry Society of India, and Sahitya Akademi. She has been reading her poems in India and abroad. Her poems have been translated into Hindi, Bengali, Urdu, Slovene, Hebrew, and Spanish. She has received awards for poetry from Green Tara Initiatives, 2018, and from All India Qaumi Ekta Manch, 2019.

Shruti Sareen studied in Rajghat Besant School KFI, Varanasi, and went on to do English literature from Indraprastha College for Women, University of Delhi. With a keen interest in Indian Poetry in English, her MPhil looks at the depiction of urban spaces whereas she has submitted a PhD on twenty-first century feminist poetry at the University of Delhi. She also teaches whenever she manages to find a job. She has earlier had her poetry by *The Little Magazine, Muse India, Reading Hour, The Literary Nest, Lakeview International Journal, Indian Cultural Forum, The Seven Sisters Post, The Chay Magazine (gender and sexuality), Ultra Violet (gender and sexuality), Brown Critique, E-Fiction India, Scripts (LGBT journal), Thumb Print Magazine, North East Review, Allegro, , Coldnoon Diaries, Kritya,* and *Vayavya*. She has had short fiction accepted for *Marked By Scorn*: an international anthology on non-normative love, *Six Seasons Review,* and another for an anthology by Queer Ink publishers. She is passionate about poetry, music, teaching, Assamese culture, queer love and sexuality, nature and the environment. She blogs at www.shrutanne-heartstrings.blogspot.com.

Smeetha Bhoumik's art has been shown in interesting exhibitions around the world. Her recent poetry features in literary journals like *Muse India* (curated by Prof. Gjv Prasad in 2017 and 2018), *Life & Legends* (2018), *Miombo Literary Voices* (2019), *Neesah* (2016), an international anthology titled *Writing Language, Culture and Development, Africa Vs Asia* (volume 1, Mwanaka, 2018), an international anthology *Muffled Moans Unleashed* (Authorspress, 2018); *Different Truths, The Ghazal Page* (2019), and others. Her recent collection of poems, *Where I Belong - Moments, Mist & Song,* has just been published (Mwanaka Publishers, 2019). Smeetha is the Founder of Women Empowered-

India (WE) and Chief Editor of *EquiVerse Space - A Sound Home in Words*, the inaugural creative writing anthology from WE. WE has just launched the first of its WE Poetry Series: *REVERIE - Into the Light* by Neha Mishra Jha.

Dr. **Srividya Sivakumar** is a poet, teacher, columnist, and speaker. Her second book of poems, *The Heart is an Attic*, is published by Hawakal Publishers, Kolkata. The book debuted as the #1 New Release in Indian Literature on Amazon.com in March 2018, and is in its second edition. Her first collection of verses, *The Blue Note,* was published by Writers Workshop, Kolkata. Her poems feature in *Epiphanies and Last Realizations of Love* (2019), Best Indian Poetry 2018, and '40 under 40'. Her poem 'Bamboo' from the *Ethos Journal* has been nominated for the Best of the Net Anthology in 2018. From February 2014 to December 2016, Srividya wrote a weekly column - Running on Poetry - for *The Hindu*'s *Metroplus*. A teacher-trainer for twenty years, Srividya has a Ph.D. in English Literature, an M.S. in Education Management, and a post-graduate diploma in Advertising and Communication.

Sudeep Sen [www.sudeepsen.org] is widely recognised as "one of the finest younger English-language poets in the international literary scene" (*BBC Radio*), who is "fascinated not just by language but the possibilities of language" (*Scotland on Sunday*). At the 2004 Struga Poetry Festival (Macedonia), he received the 'Pleiades' honour for having made "a significant contribution to contemporary world poetry". His prize-winning books include: *Postmarked India: New & Selected Poems* (HarperCollins), *Distracted Geographies, Rain, Aria* (A K Ramanujan Translation Award), *Fractals: New & Selected Poems | Translations 1980-2015 (London Magazine Editions), EroText (Vintage: Penguin Random House), and Kaifi Azmi: Poems | Nazms (Bloomsbury)*. He has edited important anthologies: *The HarperCollins Book of English Poetry, World English Poetry,* and *Modern English Poetry by Younger Indians* (Sahitya Akademi). Sen's works have been translated into over 25 languages and some have appeared in the *Times Literary Supplement, Newsweek, Guardian, Observer, Independent, Telegraph, Financial Times, Herald, Literary Review, Harvard Review, Hindu, Hindustan Times, Outlook, India Today,* and broadcast on bbc, pbs, cnn ibn, ndtv, air & *Doordarshan.* Sen's newer work appears in *New Writing 15* (Granta), *Language for a New Century* (Norton), *Love Poems* (Knopf/Everyman), *Out of Bounds* (Bloodaxe), *Initiate: Oxford New Writing* (Blackwell), and *Name me a Word* (Yale). He is the editorial director of aark arts and the editor of *Atlas.* Sen is the first Asian to read his poetry and deliver the Derek Walcott Lecture at the Nobel Laureate Festival. The Government of India's Ministry of Culture has awarded him the senior fellowship for "outstanding persons in the field of culture/literature."

Sumana Roy is the author of *How I Became a Tree*, a work of nonfiction, *Missing: A Novel,* and *Out of Syllabus: Poems.*

Tapaswinee Mitra is a 20 year old student of History, with a Bachelors in it from Jadavpur University. She is interested in the question of gender in conflict areas, and wants to pursue research in that field. You can write to her at mtapaswinee@gmail.com.

Temidayo Jacob (Mayor Jake) is a sociologist who writes from the north-central part of Nigeria. He explores real life experiences and societal happenings in his writings. His works have appeared and are forthcoming in *Rattle, Kalahari Review, Peeking Cat Poetry, Art and Rebellion, Words Rhymes and Rhythms, Ngiga Review, Inskpired* and others. He is also a contributor to leading anthologies.

Urna Bose is an advertising professional. Urna started her career in advertising as a copywriter. Having worked with some of the most well-known advertising giants in Mumbai, Urna went on to became a Creative Director and an Executive Creative Director, thereafter. Urna has been the brain-child behind a vast body of clutter-breaking, innovative and iconic advertisements and her ad-campaigns have won many creativity awards. She also writes poetry and her poetry has been published and featured in many anthologies. Urna loves travelling, and her obsessive, unapologetic wanderlust makes her dabble with travel writing, every now and then. Urna lives with her family in Mumbai, India.

photo credit: *tmn*

SOMRITA URNI GANGULY

www.ingramcontent.com/pod-product-compliance
Lightning Source LLC
LaVergne TN
LVHW041222080426
835508LV00011B/1046